HOW TO WIN OVER

Fear

A practical formula for successful living

JOHN HAGGAI

HARVEST HOUSE PUBLISHERS
Eugene, Oregon 97402

Except where otherwise indicated, all Scripture quotations in this book are taken from the King James Version of the Bible.

Scriptures marked NKJV are from the Holy Bible, New King James Version, Copyright © 1979, 1980, 1982 by Thomas Nelson, Inc. Used by permission.

Contents

HOW TO
WIN
OVER

Fear

Introduction

I'm Afraid—You're Afraid

Let's face it—we're all afraid.

No human being is immune to this most basic of emotions. In fact, it is an emotion we share with many members of the animal kingdom. But unlike animals—who seem to fear only definite and immediate threats—we can fear threats that have never been made, even threats that will never come into existence. It is possible for us to be afraid of something, like a newspaper, that by its very nature poses no threat at all!

The human being is capable of fearing almost anything. Naturally, some fears are more common than others. A recent study by Illinois Institute of Technology revealed that middle-class Americans tend to fear financial problems (losing their jobs, paying the bills, and so on), the deterioration of their health, and difficulties in social, business, and marriage relationships.

For such people—and that probably includes most of us—fear often does little more than nag the subconscious, giving them a vague feeling of disquiet about their home or their finances. Yet for many, fear has grown like a tree until it overshadows them from morning till night. Did you know that phobia, the severest form of fear, affects no less than 13 million Americans, qualifying it as the country's number two health problem? "Next to marital difficulties, alcohol and drug problems, phobias are the most common reason we see people," says Richard A. Chaifetz, president of Chicago's Comprehensive Psychological Centers (quoted in *Business Week*, April 21, 1986).

Of course, not all fear is bad. As we shall see, there is such a thing as legitimate fear, and this is not only permissible, but essential to self-preservation. The real subject of this book is illegitimate fear—fear that serves no useful purpose and wrecks the lives of those who suffer from it. Fear of this sort, whether it is mild or acute, is about as useful to you as a toothache. Putting up with it is like trying to run the 800 meters with lead weights on your back.

I tell you frankly: You will never succeed in achieving your goals while you are hampered with fear. I'll give you an example.

Fighting fear

At the age of 62, I made a promise to myself: I was going to learn how to ski.

I'd wanted to do it for years. I don't mean that sedate form of the sport called cross-country skiing, either. In a way, I would have preferred that—it's safer. But the little voice inside me said, "No. It's downhill skiing or none at all. You're going to go flying down the slope with the best of them."

I swallowed hard and gave in. I got in contact with John Bolten, a friend of mine who lives in Germany, and told him my plans.

"Are you serious?"

"Yes. Now what do I do?"

"Get a ski instructor."

"Where?"

"Austria. The best ski instructors are Austrian."

I told him I'd set aside some time to visit Austria, and he offered to arrange the details of the venture. I don't mind telling you I was scared stiff! But I was also excited, and after a few days I had told so many people that I couldn't back out without doing serious damage to my credibility.

They didn't encourage me. For every person who sounded pleased at my taking up the challenge, there were at least 20 others who tried to talk me out of it. The range of arguments they used was stunning. They began by appealing to my instinct of self-preservation. "Your muscle tone isn't what it used to be, John," said one. "If you get on that ski slope, you'll be going so slow some speedy downhill skier will hit you like you're a brick wall." Another added gravely, "You will doubtlessly break a leg."

When I resisted those ideas, they started in on my conscience. "John, if you fall over and you're laid up in a plaster cast, what's going to happen to your ministry? Don't you think it's ridiculous for a man of your age to try to act like a teenager?" And: "Do you really think this is consistent with your reputation as a mature leader who has written a major book on leadership? Won't this ridiculous project you're so determined to undertake destroy your credibility?"

Of course they were right, but my plans were already being noised abroad. Even if the compulsion left me, which it showed no signs of doing, it was too late to go back now. My only option was to control my fear by taking every precaution I could.

I called John Bolten.

"What can I do to minimize the risk of injury?"

"Get your legs in shape. It's important that your legs be in first-class shape."

So every day I got on my Air Dyne Schwinn bicycle and peddled for 30 minutes at a time. In a few months my legs were in better shape than they had been in for years.

But I was still feeling afraid.

I decided to employ self-affirmations.

"I have the genes," I told myself. "My father played tennis until he was 85. My grandfather competed in ice-skating contests on the Charles River in Boston when he was nearly 70. I can learn to downhill ski.

"Mastering the art of downhill skiing will not only give me a lift, but it will encourage many of my vegetating friends to undertake a more vigorous lifestyle.

"Learning to downhill ski will give me greater rapport with young people whom I am trying to influence for world evangelism.

"Since I won't be able to think about anything but the skiing when I'm on that slope, it will be a good activity to relax me after months of sustained and concentrated work."

There was no aid that I did not make use of. Every time I had the opportunity, I watched television programs on downhill skiing. I read articles in magazines, looking hard at the pictures and impressing them on my mind.

I bought a book on skiing, written by four news reporters from the British paper, *The Sunday Times.* People like William F. Buckley said it was one of the best books ever written on the subject. I read it carefully. I read about skis, ski boots, and ski clothing. I read every word from beginning to end. I read about the snowplow procedure for stopping. I read about the "stem christie" and the "grand wedel." I read about how to get up when you fall down and about ski etiquette.

In addition, I talked to everybody I could think of who skied. I asked them, "What's the single most important thing to remember about downhill skiing?"

They told me always to keep the weight on the downhill ski, to keep the point of the uphill ski just a little bit ahead of the point of the downhill ski, to face down the fall line, and to put your hips into the mountain. Did it make sense to me? Not exactly, but I listened hard.

I did everything I could think of to overwhelm the fear of the task to which I'd set myself. I even went to orthopedic specialists to get their input regarding the project I was about to undertake. Ironically, the specialists were the most encouraging!

Finally, 12 months after I had first phoned John Bolten, I arrived on the Austrian ski slopes. I was greatly encouraged by the applause of my wife and friends, who noted out loud even very slight improvements in my style, and expressed the conviction that I was learning fast and would ski well. At the age of 63, I became a downhill skier.

So when I say that fear stands in the way of achievement, I am speaking from my own experience. Any important undertaking, from writing a book to learning how to ski, comes with a price tag attached, and that price is measured in the currency of fear.

It is sometimes said that fear diminishes as you grow in experience. In a way that is true, because a very basic human fear is fear of the unknown, and so what has become familiar to us will also be less likely to make us afraid. But fear never vanishes entirely, and curiously enough that is really an advantage.

I remember talking in 1966 to the late Dr. William Culbertson, then president of the Moody Bible Institute. I said, "Dr. Culbertson, I'm 42 years old. I've preached around the world. I've pastored churches. Yet to this day, I don't know what it's like to get up before a group of five people—let alone five thousand—without getting the butterflies in my stomach."

"Thank God," Dr. Culbertson boomed. "When the time comes that you no longer have the butterflies, stop preaching. God will be through with you."

You see, fear has its uses. It is like a guard standing at the gate of opportunity. Every time we wish to take advantage of an opportunity, we have to overcome the guard. Maybe you think God is making life unnecessarily hard for us by barring our way like that. I don't think so. Fear may be dangerous, but it also teaches us to value what we aim for. "If it ain't worth fighting for, it ain't worth having." Fear puts us on the alert and forces us to give of our best. Like the seasoned opera star, we need it at the threshold of every performance.

Be warned, therefore. It is not my intention in writing this book to help you eliminate fear. I couldn't do that even if I wanted to, for God has so arranged things that fear will always be standing guard at the gate of opportunity, whether we like it or not. My aim is not to remove the guard once and for all, but to show you how to overcome him at each new conflict and so achieve your goals. Learning this method of "combat" by internalizing the principles taught in the Bible will give you the mastery every time.

Before you begin

Fear is probably the greatest cause of wasted potential. How many people down through the ages failed to achieve because they turned back from opportunity at first sight of the guard? If you have not read the book *Profiles in Courage* by former President John F. Kennedy, I suggest you read it. You will see what benefits accrued to the United States and to the world as a result of six men mastering fear.

My own favorite example of the victory over fear is Mother Teresa, the tiny nun from Yugoslavia whose heart is big enough to include people of every rank, intellect, culture, and creed. Her life is a parable of the mastery of fear. Fear of poverty, fear of disease, fear for personal safety, fear of being misunderstood.

In 1986, Mr. Ed Stanley, the outgoing president of the Young Presidents' Organization sent me a transcript of Mother Teresa's address to the YPO convocation. So powerful was the impact of this frail little lady on those men and women (who represent the world's business leadership under 50 years of age) that scores of them said they could never be the same. They said they planned to return to their homes and implement the challenge Mother Teresa had delivered to them by precept and example.

Ask yourself now what challenge God wants *you* to take up—a challenge that will enrich your life and honor God—which lies beyond your reach because of fear.

There is no shortage of challenges available. Businesses need to be established. Schools need to be founded. Churches need to be planted. Books need to be written. Laws need to be enacted. Vaccines need to be discovered. Pollution needs to be controlled. Who knows? You may be just the person to meet one of these needs, or one of a thousand others.

Whatever your challenge is, I pray that this book will encourage you to work toward the mastery of fear and the fulfillment of your unique potential.

"Are you sure it'll work?" you ask. The answer is yes, I am sure. Sure, that is, provided you satisfy one basic condition. A close family friend said to me, after reading *How to Win Over Worry*, "I read your book, but I still worry."

I chuckled and said, "How many times did you read it?"

"Once."

"Do you really believe that reading the book once, at the age of 53, is going to correct a habit pattern you've been developing over more than half a century?"

She said she got the point. I hope she did—and I hope you get it as well. Reading this book once will not wave a magic wand over your fears and liberate you from bondage to them. I suggest you read and reread it. I suggest you make notes in the margin or inside the back cover about passages that have a special relevance to you. I suggest you write out specific goals and time targets to help you apply its methods.

You would do well to take a hint from Paul J. Meyer of Waco, Texas, founder of Success Motivation Institute and the acknowledged authority on self-motivation. He says of his courses: "If you expose yourself daily to this material, you will gain the benefit of one of the most powerful learning techniques known—spaced repetition. An idea very seldom is absorbed the first time it is presented. To become a usable part of you, ideas must be presented over and over. Psychologists estimate that most ideas are presented at least six times before they are fully accepted and internalized."

Meyer produces his material in both audiocassettes and written manuals. He instructs his clients to listen to each cassette, one at a time every day for six days before going on to the next. That's in addition to reading the same material twice a week. If they can do both at the same time, so much the better.

There's no cassette on sale with this book. But that shouldn't keep you from picking out the passages most important to you and making your own cassettes. If you can get the information going in through your ears as well as your eyes you will learn from it more efficiently. I doubt if you will be able to read or hear "enough." A book that has made a revolutionary change in my life and work is one I have read through 13 times. I've read some chapters scores of times, and one chapter 100 times!

To start with, though, I advise you to read this book through fairly quickly, just enough to familiarize yourself with it and to get the gist of the argument. You will find further instructions at the end, but don't bother about those for the time being.

Please do not use this book as a replacement for the Bible. I heartily recommend that you devote the first moments of every day to reading the Bible, a book that is more important to your mastery of fear than any other. To help you, you may want to secure a Bible concordance, look up the word "fear" and make a study of the passages that deal with it. You will find I identify some of the main passages later on.

I wish you well. As I write this book, I pray that God will use it to help and bless you. Should you have questions about anything I've written, please write me at Box 13, Atlanta, Georgia 30370. I will answer your query. God bless you.

Part 1

LIVING DANGEROUSLY

1

Fear in Focus

A fundamental human fear is the fear of the unknown. What we cannot predict, explain, or understand is likely to make us afraid. That is why children are afraid of the dark and cautious of strangers—both present situations over which they have no control, and in which the love of those they trust does not protect them.

Adults also experience fear of the unknown. Consider the scare caused by AIDS, a viral infection scantily understood at the time of this writing, over which medicine has little control, and against the progress of which loved ones are powerless to intervene. Typhoid, cholera, and leprosy do not induce the same fear as AIDS because they are known diseases—medical science has examined them and found cures which, at least in the West, are available to sufferers. At the present time there is no cure for AIDS. In that sense it is unknown. Consequently it is an object of fear. People lose their jobs and are ostracized by former colleagues because they carry the AIDS virus.

There are many less dramatic examples than AIDS of our fear of the unknown. In a way, nearly every fear we have involves the fear of the unknown, as every fear is rooted in the future, and no one can predict with certainty what is going to happen in the next minute, let alone the next week or year. I expect you've had the experience of fearing some future event and then, when it came, finding it wasn't half as bad as you expected. The object of our fear is usually less intimidating when seen face-to-face than it is when projected in the imagination. A friend of mine, who dislikes injections and was horrified at the thought of having an inoculation for polio, was relieved to step into the doctor's office and be given a drop of serum on a lump of sugar!

Understanding what was previously unknown can go a long way to dispelling fear, as my friend found out. But understanding does something else too—it helps to solve the problem to which the fear has become attached. Understanding is 90 percent of the solution to any problem—ask anyone who's taken an exam in mathematics! It is true in all areas of life. The administrator who understands what is causing the cantankerous behavior of a staff member is 90 percent of the way to sorting it out. The golfer who understands what is causing him to slice is 90 percent of the way to correcting his swing.

It stands to reason that if a fear is linked to a specific problem, as it is with AIDS, fear will be countered by understanding. AIDS will only be an object of fear as long as science is baffled by it. Once a cure or a vaccine is found, it will no longer be feared. In fact, it may be regarded with insufficient caution, as other veneral diseases have often been since the introduction of penicillin.

What is true for individual fears is also true for fear in general.

Your particular fears may or may not involve the unknown. Either way, you can be sure that those fears are made worse, not by the unknownness of the thing you fear (you may be well acquainted with it!), but by the unknownness of fear as an entity. Say your fear is in the area of personal finance and you are afraid of losing your job or of not being able to make ends meet. The chances are you already know a lot about employment prospects at your place of work, and the options open to you through the services of a bank. But how much do you know about fear?

I would guess not much. We tend to experience fear rather than analyze it. Yet I've just said that understanding a problem is 90 percent of the solution. And isn't fear a problem? If it is, we would be well advised to study it before we go much further. And that is why the first two sections of this book are about the nature and effects of fear.

How fear fits in

The first recorded case of fear in the Bible comes in the early chapters of Genesis. Until their sin, Adam and Eve lived in harmony with God and with the rest of the created order. The economy of life for prefallen man was supremely simple: he was to have dominion over all living creatures, and all living creatures were to be given vegetation for food. Genesis pictures an idyllic pastoral scene in which man and woman carry out their twin responsibilities to worship God and look after His creation:

> God blessed them, and God said unto them, Be fruitful, and multiply, and replenish the earth, and subdue it: and have dominion over the fowl of the air, and over every living thing that moveth upon the earth.
> And God said, Behold I have given you every herb bearing seed, which is upon the face of all the earth, and every tree in which is the fruit of a tree yielding seed; to you it shall be for meat. And to every beast of the earth, and to every fowl of the air, and to every thing that creepeth upon the earth, wherein there is life, I have given every green herb for meat: and it was so (Genesis 1:28-30).

What follows is that Adam and Eve destroyed their communion with God through disobedience. In that, they stand as symbols for every human being who has ever lived.

But notice the changing role of fear in the story of the Fall. In their prefallen state, the only fear Adam and Eve knew was the mild and useful fear that all good men have in the face of justice. We might call it "respect." As long as they inclined their freedom to the love of God, the prohibition against eating from the tree of knowledge affected them no more than we are affected by the death penalty for murder. If we are responsible citizens, we don't refrain from murdering someone because murder is against the law. We refrain because it is in our nature to refrain—conscience makes the act abhorrent to us. In a society made up entirely of responsible citizens, the law against murder would be unnecessary because nobody would want to kill.

So it was in Eden. By nature Adam and Eve had no appetite for the forbidden fruit.

But appetite can be aroused. We haven't all been tempted to pick up a gun and shoot somebody, but none of us can deny having experienced the temptation to retaliate. And it is once we have been provoked that fear begins to operate. When somebody insults you, it isn't usually humility that keeps you quiet (most people would love to lay their detractors out cold!). You suffer in silence for fear of embarrassing others or making yourself look like a fool. It is exactly the same mechanism that makes the penal code a deterrent to crime. In a society with no punishment, crime will be committed with insolence; but where crime is punishable, the criminal will think twice before breaking the law.

It is significant that when he tempts Eve, the serpent starts by *assuming* her compliance: "Yea, hath God said, Ye shall not eat of every tree in the garden?" (Genesis 3:1). He hints strongly that this was an unreasonable demand for God to make, and Eve falls for the suggestion hook, line, and sinker. Instead of affirming her belief in God's commands and replying, "Yes, He has said that, and I agree with Him," she allows herself to take the serpent's standpoint. In effect she says, "I don't know why, but God doesn't want us eating from the tree of knowledge, and since He will punish me if I do, I'm not going to go near it."

She is wide open. She has declared that her obedience stands on fear, and not on her natural goodness. Mentally she has already fallen; all that separates her from the act of disobedience is her fear of retribution. This fear the serpent is swift to allay:

> The serpent said unto the woman, Ye shall not surely die (Genesis 3:4).

Having soothed her fear (and no doubt she was very willing to have it soothed), he proceeds to whet her appetite a little more, and with no fear left to deter her she soon falls, dragging her husband after her. But the result is ironic—their newfound knowledge, far from raising them to the promised equality with God, only returns them to a state of subjection. In their innocent fear of God they had enjoyed limitless freedom. Now that they have tried to take God's place, it is fear that calls the tune:

> The eyes of them both were opened, and they knew that they were naked; and they sewed fig leaves together, and made themselves aprons.
>
> And they heard the voice of the Lord God walking in the garden in the cool of the day: and Adam and his wife hid themselves from the presence of the Lord God amongst the trees of the garden. And the Lord God called unto Adam, and said until him, Where art thou?
>
> And he said, I heard thy voice in the garden, and I was afraid, because I was naked; and I hid myself.
>
> And he said, Who told thee that thou wast naked? Hast thou eaten of the tree, whereof I commanded thee that thou shouldest not eat?
>
> And the man said, The woman whom thou gavest to be with me, she gave me of the tree, and I did eat.
>
> And the Lord God said unto the woman, What is this that thou hast done? And the woman said, The serpent beguiled me and I did eat (Genesis 3:7-13).

Adam and Eve had never before known what it was to be afraid. But this shift in their experience of fear was a natural result of their disobedience. I use the word "natural" because just as in their prefallen state it was "natural" for them to know God as a benefactor, so after the Fall it was "natural" for them to know Him as a judge. One act of disobedience was enough to fix the abyss of sin between them and the Creator.

Now that the abyss was in place the threat of retribution was no longer remote; it was immediate, tangible, real. For the first time they had something to fear. Hence the fig leaves and the frantic passing of the buck.

We might note that all of the fear referred to in the Eden story was legitimate; that is, it all served a useful purpose. Even the fear that made Adam and Eve hide from God was legitimate—after all, the judgment of God is not to be taken lightly. However, Adam and Eve's reaction reveals something more basic about fear, something that characterizes fear in all its forms.

It is this: fear does not exist in isolation. It is a *response to danger.*

The dependence of fear on danger is made clear in its very definition. Merriam-Webster's dictionary describes fear as "an unpleasant emotion caused by the anticipation or aware-ness of danger." You can never be scared, as it were, in the abstract: you are always scared of *something* even if you cannot say precisely what that something is.

The first point to learn about fear, then, is that it is a God-given potential designed for our protection. Eve would not have felt the deterrent power of God's command in Eden if she had not already possessed the faculty of fear. True, as long as they remained in a state of innocence, Adam and Eve had no practical use for this faculty. But they did not remain in innocence. And at the moment that intuitive harmony with God and the natural environment disappeared, when the first couple was cast out of Paradise and the ground was cursed through their sin, fear became not only a possibility but a necessity.

Today, as Ashley Montagu aptly expressed it, "to be human is to be in danger." He might have said, "to be alive is to be in danger," because fear is not the exclusive property of human beings. Fear—the basic, physiological response that increases the heart rate in readiness for flight or defensive action—affects the wild beast fleeing from the leopard, just as it affects me when I see another driver about to run into my car. The response is instinctive and essential. And incidentally it gives rise to many of the euphemisms we use to describe fear, such as "gooseflesh" or "the shivers":

> The heart beats faster. Breathing is accelerated, and the glands are stimulated to greater activity. The muscles become taut, preparing for struggle or flight. A strain is placed on the whole physical system. . . . Fear is an elemental alarm system. It is an indispensable part of our means of self-preservation. A fearless man would have difficulty remaining alive for a single day in the tangled confusion of traffic in any large metropolitan city (G. Ernest Thomas, *Faith Can Master Fear*).

Fearless men, in fact, frequently do come to grief. A farmer living downwind from Mount Saint Helens had been warned of the possible eruption of the volcano and refused to move. He perished. So, too, did 300 residents of Cameron, Louisiana, who defied a flood warning.

So I am not going to tell you to get rid of your faculty of fear. You need it to tell you when you are in danger. In this uncertain world, fear is a gift to be thankful for. Fear may be unpleasant. But if it wasn't, you wouldn't take any notice of it!

So get it into your head right now that fear in *itself* is an asset. It is there to put you in a physical and mental state where you are most capable of tackling whatever danger is ahead of you. Think how useful fear is when there's a man behind you with a gun in his hand! And think also how useful fear is on a societal level. After all, it is fear that is largely responsible for adequate defense arrangements. Certainly fear lay behind the provision of hospitals and sanitariums for the treatment of tuberculosis in the early years of this century. It is probably doing the same now for research into the treatment of AIDS.

Be realistic

You will never be able to escape from danger. To attempt to do so is pointless and counterproductive. Danger will confront you in any enterprise you engage in, and wherever danger is, there will be fear. The person who avoids danger because he doesn't like fear will not be fulfilling his potential. As I pointed out earlier, sidestepping fear means sidestepping the challenge of life and passing up the opportunity of achievement. Of course, fear is a nasty experience. But the answer is not to avoid it, but to use, transcend, and overcome it. How else did Sir Edmund Hillary get to the top of Mount Everest, or Neil Armstrong to the moon? How else has anyone achieved anything that involved more risk than spilling ink on his pants?

But maybe you don't want to face up to your fear. In that case, two options are open to you.

One option is to cut and run. To cop out. To avoid places, people, and situations that stimulate fear. That was what Adam and Eve were doing hiding among the trees. They were trying to put off the dreadful moment when they would have to confront God. Of course, it didn't work. Fear will nearly always track you down in the end. But even if it doesn't, the chances are you will fall into a fear far worse than the one you are trying to escape from. Remember what happened to Jonah? God told him to go and preach to the Ninevites, and Jonah, calculating that the Ninevites would have him for breakfast if he turned up denouncing their wickedness, promptly set off in the opposite direction.

But God refused to let him off the hook:

> The Lord sent out a great wind into the sea, and there was a mighty tempest in the sea, so that the ship was like to be broken. . . . So they took up Jonah, and cast him forth (Jonah 1:4,15).

In the end, Jonah was persuaded to go to Nineveh, and the whole city repented in dust and ashes. Jonah was running not just from his fear, but from God, which explains why God put such a terrifying obstacle in his way. But the conclusion of the story gives hope to any fearful person. Whoever is following God's way can expect God's help. If you are serious in reading this book, therefore, and serious in desiring to apply its

Scriptural solution to fear, you may be assured of God's assistance. If God brought the Ninevites to repentance, He can subdue your fears.

The second option open to you is covering up—getting out the fig leaf and trying to hide your embarrassing fears from those around you. This not only fails to conceal fear, it actually makes fear worse.

I'll explain in the next chapter.

2

Three Disguises of Fear

The story of Adam and Eve tells us something we know from our own experience: fear has an insidious power over us.

When we are afraid, we are driven to perform actions alien to our usual pattern of behavior. Until fear entered their lives, it had never occurred to Adam and Eve to sew fig leaves together for clothing. Clothing had never been necessary. They turned tailor because knowledge made them ashamed. Suddenly they felt unpresentable to God, to each other, and to the outside world. As a result, they tried to disguise their nakedness with clothing.

Today, we go a step further than Adam. Adam, at least, was willing to admit his fear. When God asked him why he was hiding, he said simply, "I was afraid." Most people today try to hide not just their own perceived inadequacies, but the very fact of their fear. In a culture where the virtues of strength and courage are held in high regard, fear is a kind of inadequacy. Consequently the world is full of fearful people desperately pretending to be fearless. And let's be frank about it—it is a pretense. As long as you refuse to tackle fear at the root, it will continue to grow. And especially as you get on in years and you are faced with more legitimate objects of fear (serious illness or death, for example) the effort of pretense will become insupportable.

My mind goes back to a man about my own age whom I met in my 20's. At that time he was handsome, bright, flamboyant and, I must say, arrogant. He cut a wide swath in his peer group. He got things done. Whether you liked him or not, you could not ignore him. I met this man for the second time about ten years ago. He had changed. His wife had left him. He was hated by his children, two of whom had gotten into

He was hated by his children, two of whom had gotten into serious trouble with the law. He had been crippled with arthritis. What struck me was his quietness and sensitivity, the ease with which I could talk to him. But at the same time, I could not shake off the urge to pity him. As I said to a friend later, "I almost preferred him the way he was." Fear had worn him down.

I've seen it countless times. I've lived long enough to recognize a girl who masks her secret fears with excessive attention to her face and figure. She projects charm and vivacity. But even if she is genuinely beautiful (and girls of this sort often are), age knocks the props out from under her. The wrinkling of the skin and the changing contours of her figure gradually erode her confidence until the old fears show through.

Simon Peter wrestled with fear (read Mark 14). On the face of it, Peter was a bombastic character. He himself declared that though everyone else fall away, he would stick by Jesus to the end. When Jesus foretold Peter's betrayal Peter covered up his fears with loud assertions of loyalty: "If I should die with thee, I will not deny thee" (Mark 14:31). But when it came to the test, fear won out.

> A little after, they that stood by said again to Peter, Surely thou art one of them: for thou art a Galilean, and thy speech agreeth thereto. But he began to curse and to swear, saying, I know not this man of whom ye speak.
>
> And the second time the cock crew. And Peter called to mind the word that Jesus said unto him, Before the cock crow twice, thou shalt deny me thrice. And when he thought thereon, he wept (Mark 14:70-72).

Here is a fine example of the power of fear. Peter could brag in front of his friends, but under duress he could neither hide his fear nor stop it from controlling him. Later, in the safety of darkness, he reproached himself bitterly. Yet his betrayal was inevitable, not because he was helpless, but because he refused to be helped. In adopting a disguise for his fear he had probably fooled even himself. There is no hint of hypocrisy in his brave promise to Jesus. But by placing so much confidence in his own abilities he neglected in Gethsemane the one opportunity given to him to confront his fear instead of covering it up:

> He cometh, and findeth them sleeping, and said unto Peter, Simon, sleepest thou? Couldest not thou watch one hour? Watch ye and pray, lest ye enter into temptation. The spirit truly is ready, but the flesh is weak (Mark 14:37,38).

In the long run, disguises do nothing to remove fear, you can paint over the rust on your automobile, but paint isn't going to stop the bodywork from falling to bits. If you think it is, you are deluding yourself.

Disguises, besides being ineffective, are also harmful. They distort your personality and corrode your relationships. How could they not? When you adopt a disguise for fear, you are compensating for it by behaving in a way that is not natural to you. Would you spend the rest of your life playing the role of Othello or Lady Macbeth? Of course you wouldn't. If you did, you would soon find yourself under lock and key. Yet there are millions of people today walking around so heavily disguised that, ironically, the first thought that comes to a person who meets them is that they're trying to hide something. The disguise misfires. It is meant to manipulate the responses of others, but it only undermines the mutual love and trust that are essential for a balanced relationship.

Fear has three common disguises: strength, saintliness, and love.

The disguise of strength

This was Peter's disguise. Fear masquerading as strength seeks to impress others with feats of daring, and to create the illusion of competence by projecting a powerful personality.

There is nothing wrong with a powerful personality, and not all men and women who come across like that are trying to conceal fear. Strength of character is a mark of the Spirit, even in those who by nature are quiet and reserved. As Paul said of himself, "When I am weak, then am I strong" (2 Corinthians 12:10). This authentic power, though it organizes and motivates effectively, is never overbearing. The powerful personality adopted as a disguise, however, will come across to others as a desire for domination. It doesn't motivate, it suffocates.

Consequently it is self-defeating. The fearful person suspects a gulf between himself and his fellows, and because he doesn't have the assurance that issues from a spirit dominated by the Spirit, he tries to compensate for his own lack of self-confidence by dominating others. This sets up a tension between his real self (the self that wants to be loved and accepted) and his assumed self (the self that projects bravado for purposes of manipulation). It also fails to achieve its objective. You cannot force another person to give you love and acceptance, for the more strength you display, the more likely you are to drive him away from you. And so the fear intensifies. I am not joking—I have seen men of wealth and prominence attempting to overcome their fear by hiring public relations men to "puff" them. I've watched them act with unwarranted aggression toward their employees. They have taken these measures to disguise fear. They will go to ludicrous lengths to curry the favor of the public.

The man or woman disguising fear with strength is doomed to unhappiness. Compare Paul with Nero. The apostle Paul suffered appalling hardship for the gospel. For the greater part of his life he was on the run, in prison, or in danger of being killed. "Surely," you say, "he would have been more content had he experienced the blessings enjoyed by Nero— wealth, influence, and an almost limitless circle of admirers." Yet you would have to go a long way to find a happier man than Paul. And Nero, who craved Rome's acclamation, not only as its finest emperor, but also as its most talented musician and charioteer, died by his own hand at 32, a frustrated dissolute.

A fearful person using the disguise of strength suffers terrifying symptoms.

1. *He can never be himself.* Projecting strength leaves him in a state of perpetual competition. He must always go one better if he's going to retain the admiration of those around him. And if he's going to do that, he's also forced to conform to their standards—otherwise, there is no basis on which to judge the winner. So he is enslaved by the lifestyle of his peers. He sends his children to their school, drives their make of car, and wears their brand of clothing. He builds a summer home on the same lake, joins the same clubs, and goes on the same tours. He is not free to fulfill his own potential, and when he encounters people who are, he can only respond by trying to belittle them.

2. *He can never enjoy his success.* He is driven to move for the sake of moving, to strive for the sake of striving, and above all to keep ahead in competition with his peers. There is no chance for him to take a rest, to look back on all he has done and, without reference to anybody else, enjoy his achievement for its own sake. His habit of activity will drive him, even in the absence of defined goals. Having nothing to aim for, he doubles his activity, and often ends up dropping dead of a heart attack.

3. *He can never enjoy others.* He is too busy evaluating them, measuring them, and comparing them to himself. He would take no pleasure in others anyway. He wants them not for who they are, but for what they can give to him.

4. *He can never be satisfied.* If the person living on bravado survives long enough, he will eventually be forced to slow down. And when he has time on his hands to think, he will likely be devastated by a sense of failure. He has fortified his confidence by demeaning his underlings and gloating on the downfall of his superiors. He has not admitted that he was afraid. But what has he achieved that will be of any lasting

value, or even of fleeting satisfaction to him? And what has he done to himself? Paul wrote to Timothy that he must "not quarrel but be gentle to all, able to teach, patient, in humility correcting those who are in opposition . . ." (2 Timothy 2:24,25 NKJV). That is a strength of character bravado will never produce.

The disguise of saintliness

If strength comes across to the outsider as domination, saintliness comes across as sanctimoniousness.

Of course, there is a proper saintliness. The word translated "saint" in the New Testament actually means "set apart," so strictly speaking a saint is anyone, lay or ordained, male or female, liturgical or nonliturgical, who is set apart by the indwelling life of Christ for a life of service—in other words, any Christian. It is hoped that every Christian will also be saintly in the common sense of the term, that is, outstandingly virtuous.

However, there is the world of difference between being saintly in this sense (as evidence of the work of the Spirit) and appearing saintly (for the sake of impressing others). Appearing saintly is a popular way of disguising fear. It is also good for concealing a host of other unpleasant traits, as tricksters, charlatans, and dishonest salesmen down the ages have been delighted to discover.

How doth the little crocodile
  Improve his shining tail
And pour the waters of the Nile
  On every golden scale!

How cheerfully he seems to grin,
  How neatly spreads his claws,
And welcomes little fishes in
  With gently smiling jaws!
                    —Lewis Carroll
                    Alice in Wonderland

If you are in the business of looking saintly, you will find yourself in good company. Paul blows the whistle on a few aspiring "saints" in 2 Corinthians:

> Such are false apostles, deceitful workers, transforming themselves into the apostles of Christ. And no marvel; for Satan himself is transformed into an angel of light. Therefore it is no great thing if his ministers also be transformed as the ministers of righteousness; whose end shall be according to their works (2 Corinthians 11:13-15).

But wait a minute, you say. Surely Paul is talking here about the unregenerate? Of course he is. But if the devil can daub himself in greasepaint and pass himself off as an angel, think how much easier it is for a Christian, under the influence of fear, to mimic the appearance of virtue!

I'll let you in on a secret. You can nearly always spot this phony saintliness—all you have to do is see how it is expressed. False virtue gives itself away by telling you, not what it does, but what it *doesn't* do. When I was a boy, I learned to spot a phony saint a mile off. Many church people I knew considered themselves dedicated Christians on the strength of their abstinence. They didn't drink. They didn't smoke. They didn't dance, play cards, or go to movies. But you should have seen some of them in church! They could lie, cheat, covet, and even split congregations in two with their fractious spirits.

Their list of official sins was ridiculously selective. Apparently they had never studied the works of the flesh Paul enumerates in Galatians 5:19-21. If they had they would have seen that 11 of the 18 he names are sins of attitude. The very projection of saintliness is a form of deception, and therefore a sin. It was exactly that sin for which Ananias and Sapphira lost their lives in the early church (Acts 5:1-10). Nobody would have blamed them for holding back part of their estate. But to hold back part, when they pretended to have given it all, was gross dishonesty.

I am in no doubt that fear lies at the root of much assumed saintliness. How many times have I been in a church business meeting when some headstrong, stubborn-willed trouble-maker has stood up and said, "As I prayed, the Lord told me that this is the action we must take. . . ." A person like that is using his saintly reputation to manipulate others. He lines up his opinion in such a way that anyone opposing him seems to be opposing the will of God. He may deserve the good reputa-tion he has. But no degree of spirituality or success can turn a man into an oracle. If he thinks it can, then he has uncon-sciously fallen victim to his own public relations, and now that he sits on the top of the pile, he cannot bear the thought of being voted down, criticized, or given bad press. In short, he is afraid.

Fear disguised as saintliness degrades the personality in several ways.

Through pride. Fear is proud often through dogged insis-tence of its own humility. I had a professor who had the unthinking vanity to repeat to his students in class, "Teacher is humble, teacher is humble."

Through condescension. Fear is critical, always putting others right. But the habit of using phony saintliness to criticize others ultimately brings about its own downfall. The fearful person hopes through criticizing others to secure his own position. But criticism is like a drug—the more you dole out, the more you need to dole out to achieve the same feeling of superiority. In the end, you will repulse even genuinely good and tolerant people.

Through inflexibility. When you are filled with fear and endeavoring to cover up with saintliness, flexibility is diffi-cult, if not impossible. Any deviation from your tick list of "don'ts" so threatens your sense of adequacy that you must rise up in censure.

Through unreality. A person wearing saintliness as a dis-guise has left the real world and taken flight in fantasy. In doing this, he lays a guilt trip on others who think that his saintliness is real. They think, "I could never be as good as that," without realizing they are being made to chase a mirage. In moments of rational reflection, the person may feel himself stretched across the yawning chasm between the saintliness he has assumed and the inadequacy of his real life. At that point he develops another fear—that of being found out.

It might do him good! There is no progress without honesty. As a young man visiting a country church in the Piedmont section of South Carolina, I heard a story that would have amused me had it not been so painfully true. During a Wednesday night prayer meeting at the Baptist Church, the pastor asked for testimonies. "Just stand up and tell what the Lord has done for you." One after another stood up and thanked God for His saving grace, His sustaining power, and His answers to prayer. Finally one man got up and said, "I thank God I don't cuss. I don't drink. I don't run with wild women. I don't gamble. I don't steal."

The pastor said, "Bill, we're few in number here. We know each other well. We really have no secrets from one another. Let's be honest. Let's level. What's your besetting sin?"

Bill replied: "Lying, dadburn it. Lying!"

The disguise of love

This disguise works on a more personal level than strength or saintliness. But like them it has two faces. From the inside, love used as a disguise for fear seems like generosity and self-giving. From the outside it comes across as possessiveness.

Many people are simply afraid of losing somebody close to them—usually a child or a spouse. Consequently they go out of their way to help, advise, and protect the person. A mother who has a possessive relationship with her daughter will show excessive concern about any area in which the child must eventually exercise independent judgment. She will express strong and often censorious opinions about the daughter's choice of friends, vocation, place of residence, and partner in marriage. All this is done in the name of love. She wants "the best" for her child, and will stop at nothing to get it. In reality, however, it is likely that she wants the best only for herself, and that the fear of losing her daughter drives her to influence the girl's decisions with a view to allaying her own fears.

Predictably, like strength and saintliness, this sort of "love" has the effect of actualizing fears rather than dispelling them. Possessiveness smothers. The child, deprived of her independence as she enters teenage years, desires it all the more and sees her mother as the obstacle to obtaining it. Eventually there is an argument. The daughter leaves home. The mother, who is devastated, tells herself that her love has been repaid with ingratitude, and wallows in self-pity. Yet there would have been no separation had she dealt with her fear when it first appeared. As it was, she accepted the fear, tried to disguise it with what she called love, and reaped the consequences.

The genuine article

All three disguises of fear—strength, saintliness, and love— are destructive in their effects. They produce the negative personality traits of domination, sanctimoniousness, and possessiveness, which will destroy the very relationships they were intended to protect and build. They are counterfeits crafted by fear. But the counterfeits must not be allowed to detract from the genuine virtues on which the disguises are modeled.

For that reason, I want to finish this chapter by looking briefly at the lives of three men I have been privileged to know, in whom true strength of character, true godliness, and true generosity have shone out like the sun.

Probably nobody has had a stronger influence on my life in regard to Christian giving than Guy Rutland. For one thing, he gave as much thought and preparation to his giving as he did to his business. For another, he neither sought nor needed public exposure as an incentive to give. Since his death, his family has learned of the enormous help he gave to people they knew nothing about.

Certainly no one invested more hours, more effort, and more dollars than Guy Rutland did in Haggai Institute. He served for 13 years as its treasurer. In that position, he could have exerted a lot of pressure to achieve ends inconsistent with the stated aims of the organization. He never did. In fact, this business tycoon would say, "John, we are looking to you for leadership. We believe God has sovereignly given you the vision. You make clear to us what needs to be done, and we are going to follow you to the best of our ability under the leadership of the Holy Spirit."

Another such person was Cecil Day. He died at 44, but he accomplished more in that time than most of us could achieve in a life twice as long. Though he gave enormous gifts of money, time, and influence to the Institute, not once in all the years I knew him did he display any possessiveness over its work. He refused to stifle it for his own interest.

Once we ran into a financial crisis so severe that the Institute faced closure. We needed immediate answers, so I phoned six trustees and asked them to meet me at the Executive Park Hotel in Atlanta. Amazingly—considering their heavy schedules—all six came without hesitation. After prayer and discussion, they came up with a sound solution, one that did not entail any immediate additional outlay of money from them (they were already giving to the limit). As we were walking out of the building, I remember Cecil, then 39, turning to me and saying wistfully, "I wish I had a group of men I could call on the spur of the moment, who would come up with answers like that!"

I realized then, for the first time, what a uniquely capable and consecrated group of men and women undergirded my ministry.

A third man was Arnold Browning, a wealthy hotel and real estate businessman from the Bay Area in California. He hadn't heard of the Haggai Institute until he was 61 years old. But from that time until his death at 78 he, too, gave unstintingly of his money, influence, and time. He would drop everything to arrange a meeting in the Bay Area and invite outstanding business leaders to learn about the organization. At the time of life when most men are slowing down, he was traveling as far as Singapore for the work of the Institute.

Had any one of these men been gripped by fear, the story of my ministry at the Haggai Institute might have turned out very differently. None of them were. Each of them had a strong personality. Each had impeccable financial credentials. Each acted in genuine Christian love.

Their lives are demonstrations of the victory over fear—the same victory you can have through the power of God.

Part 2

HOW SCARED ARE YOU?

3

The First Degree—Rational Fear

In the introduction to this book, I said that your fears can be classed as legitimate or illegitimate.

Legitimate fear can be a problem, but it will be a much greater and more complex problem if it has become illegitimate. But how exactly are the two distinguished? At what point does a legitimate fear become illegitimate?

The key to understanding this is the all-important relationship between fear and danger, for as we said, fear doesn't exist in a vacuum—it is a response.

Rational fear

The intensity of fear (how scared we feel) depends on two factors.

The first factor is the *level of danger* encountered. If you are young and at the peak of fitness, you will probably not fear for your health. There is no danger, nothing to be scared of. If, on the other hand, you are middle-aged and have a persistent pain in your chest, there will be cause for concern, and you will experience a corresponding level of fear. If you then consult a doctor and he says you have developed an incurable heart condition of which you are going to die in two weeks, your fear will intensify.

The greater the danger, the fiercer the warning signals the body sends to the conscious mind.

You might think that the difference between legitimate and illegitimate fear is a matter of intensity. But this is not so. If it were, high levels of danger would always make your fear illegitimate, which is nonsense. Imagine yourself walking in a forest one day and hearing a rustling sound in the undergrowth. You creep forward, hoping to catch sight of a squirrel or a fox, and then, as you push aside a branch, you get the shock of your life. It's a grizzly bear. All at once your heart jumps into your mouth, the hairs stand up on the back of your neck, and you break out in a cold sweat from head to toe. Scared? You are almost crazy with fear. If you could climb, you would already be a hundred feet up in the nearest pine tree!

Nobody could say your fear in that situation is illegitimate. It is acute, because the level of danger is acute—you're in real danger of being torn limb from limb. All those abrupt changes in your metabolism are your body's way of giving you the best possible chance of escape. If you found yourself standing ten yards from a grizzly bear and your body did not respond in that way, your chances of survival would be significantly reduced.

But what is helpful when you are face-to-face with a grizzly bear can be a handicap when you are dealing with ordinary dangers. Say you are going for a job interview. There is no threat to your life here, but you badly want the job, and there is a danger that you won't get it. As a result, your pulse rate increases, beads of perspiration form on your brow, and your throat gets so tight you can hardly speak. By the time you go into the prospective employer's office and shake hands with him, you are showing all the physiological signs of panic. You blow your chances through excessive and unnecessary fear.

The lesson is this: in order for your God-given capacity for fear to function effectively, it is necessary that the *level of fear you experience* be in proportion to the *level of danger you confront*.

This proper correspondence between fear and danger is what makes a fear legitimate. Fear that arises out of (and is appropriate to) a certain level of danger is *rational fear*. It makes an accurate assessment of the level of danger faced, and creates the conditions in which evasive action may be taken.

The role of *rational fear* in response to the nearness of a grizzly bear is obvious. But *rational fear* operates just as efficiently when the danger is mild or, statistically, a matter of chance. If you met a smaller animal than a grizzly bear in the forest, *rational fear* would still make you cautious of going too near it. *Rational fear* prevents you from walking casually along the edge of cliffs. It urges you to take out life insurance so that your family will be provided for in the event of your death. It makes you look for traffic before you cross a highway, get the right vaccinations before you travel abroad, and make prudent plans for your children's education.

Remember, fear is not wrong in itself. It is part of your survival mechanism. Provided that your fear is rational, it will always be legitimate. To be afraid of walking on thin ice is to show a just regard for the natural laws God has written into the world. To be afraid of falling ill or having an accident (to the extent that fear moves you to get medical insurance) is neither paranoia nor a lack of faith in God's providence, but the simple wisdom of precaution.

Let me give you an example.

A friend of mine said to me recently, "Travel is treacherous. The terrorists are accelerating their efforts. Your life has already been threatened in Indonesia and in Australia. You've been under house arrest in Pakistan. In the '60's, you visited an area in Afghanistan where no Americans had been invited. Don't you think you're being reckless?"

I responded: "I'll tell you what I told my son Johnny when he got so upset about my visiting Vietnam back in the '60's. 'Johnny,' I said, 'Daddy is safer in Vietnam in the will of God than in Atlanta, Georgia, out of the will of God.' "

"That may be true," my friend said. "But I've often heard you quote the wise words of the psalmist: 'Keep back thy servant also from presumptuous sins' " (Psalm 19:13).

"Okay. But since I believe that my travel is essential to carrying out my God-ordained mandate, I must go."

"Then why don't you let me provide you with some bodyguards? I'll underwrite full salary and expenses for three bodyguards, so you will have protection every hour of the day."

I thanked him for his generosity, but I wasn't moved.

"What good is a bodyguard? Did bodyguards keep President Reagan from being shot? Did bodyguards protect John Kennedy or Robert Kennedy or Martin Luther King or Moro or Somoza or Sadat?

"You may think I'm foolhardy, but I will tell you that having three bodyguards only makes you more visible. I take sensible precautions. There are usually at least two, often five or six people with me wherever I go, in different rooms of the hotel or different seats of the plane. I announce my itinerary to the appropriate people. When I'm in a country that's under the cloud of oppression or terrorism, I let the hotel staff know where I'm going, how I'm traveling, and when I expect to be back. I tell them whom to contact if I don't return at the announced time."

That is my way of dealing with the threat of terrorist reprisals. The fear is perfectly rational, but it is in proportion to the danger. If it wasn't, I'd have two bodyguards standing behind my desk as I write.

I have some less spectacular dangers to combat, too.

As a typical American, I have learned that I have a weak stomach when it comes to foreign food. Once, when I was overseas in 1969, I got so sick I thought I would die—in fact, I didn't much care if I did! As a result, whenever I'm traveling in places where I suspect my stomach will not tolerate the food, I restrict my diet to guarantee hygiene. Rice and tea are always safe because they have been boiled. So are fruits like the banana, from which you can remove the skin. I also take some toast and, occasionally, marmalade. I remember once being served a glass of Coke, which a generous waiter had loaded with ice cubes. I knew Coke would be fine, but I feared that the ice cubes might have been made with contaminated water. To be safe, I sent it back.

More recently, I went for a sophisticated medical checkup in Germany. The doctors told me I should treat myself a bit more kindly. "Get more rest," they said. "Spend more time in interesting diversions, and take more time when you travel between areas of varying climate. Try not to spend more than four or five hours flying in one 24-hour period."

Following their instructions is requiring a complete overhaul of my lifestyle. But I'm doing it. Why? Because I have a *rational fear* that if I push myself too hard I'll die before my time. The doctors said that given my genetic structure and God's blessing, I could live to be 90, like my father. But if I am going to get those extra years, I need to take care of myself so I'm fit to enjoy them.

Paul talked frankly about his fears. When he wrote to the Corinthians, "I was with you in weakness, and in fear, and in much trembling" (1 Corinthians 2:3), he did not mean that he distrusted God or was losing grip on his faith. In the next verse he says, "My speech and my preaching was not with enticing words of man's wisdom, but in demonstration of the Spirit and of power." How could he demonstrate God's power and at the same time be afraid? Easily, because his fear was a natural, God-given faculty to respond to the very real danger he was in. The pressure was constant:

> When we were come into Macedonia, our flesh had no rest, but we were troubled on every side; without were fightings, within were fears.
> Nevertheless God, that comforteth those that are cast down, comforted us by the coming of Titus (2 Corinthians 7:5,6).

For Paul, fear came with the territory of his apostolic office. We never hear him praying to be delivered from this fear. But when he asked for prayer from the Ephesians that he might fulfill his duties as an evangelist, it appears, though he doesn't say so explicitly, that he was seeking to transcend and overcome the fear of persecution.

> Pray for me, that utterance may be given unto me, that I may open my mouth boldly, to make known the mystery of the gospel, for which I am an ambassador in bonds: that therein I may speak boldly, as I ought to speak (Ephesians 6:19,20).

So *rational fear* is something we all can and should experience for our own well-being. It is what we might call the "first degree of fear," that is, fear in its normal and proper proportions. In short, it is legitimate fear. Fear in the first degree is still unpleasant. In its way, it still needs to be won over. But it does what fear is meant to do; it focuses our attention not on itself, but on the danger giving rise to it. We are more powerfully aware of the grizzly bear than we are of our terror of the grizzly bear. We are more powerfully aware of the danger of quicksand than we are of our fear of falling into it.

This is not true of fear in the second and third degrees, as we shall see. But before turning to them, I want to look briefly at two distinctions you will find helpful in examining your own fear.

Fear-objects and fear-scenarios

Whenever a fear is focused—in other words, whenever we say we are scared of something rather than just scared—we are relating our fear to some tangible object, event, or circumstance. But when we do this we may be referring to one of two things: the fear-object, or the fear-scenario. The two are so closely connected that we easily confuse them.

Suppose you tell me you have a problem with fear, and I respond by asking you what you are afraid of.

"Flying," you say.

"Okay," I reply. "Do you mean that the fact of being carried several thousand feet above the ground in an airplane is, in itself, what terrifies you?" You think for a moment and then admit that it's not. "So what scares you?" I ask.

You answer, "The thought that while I'm strapped into my seat, the plane might crash, and I'll be burned to death or suffocated by the fumes."

Although you began by saying that flying is the experience you are afraid of, it is, in fact, not flying, but crashing that you fear. Crashing (and consequently dying an unpleasant death) is the real fear-object. Flying is frightening to you not for itself, but for what it might lead to. If airplanes were, and had always been, roomy, comfortable and absolutely safe—and if bicycles were proven to be lethal—you would probably say you were scared of cycling instead. Actually, in statistical terms, you are far safer in a plane than on a bike! Nonetheless you have come to associate your fear of crashing with flying. Flying is your fear-scenario.

The tendency to confuse the fear-object with the fear-scenario is characteristic of the way fear spreads. Fear-objects are always specific. One of the horrifying features of the society portrayed in George Orwell's *1984* is the way the authorities identify personal fear-objects and then use them to torture captives—in the case of Winston Smith, with rats.

Even what we recognize as a single fear-object may, in fact, be a collection of them. Crashing in an airplane, for example, involves several fears: the fear of death, the fear of pain, the fear of confinement, and so on. We are justified in calling the crash a fear-object because it is an event in which those particular fears will almost certainly be realized. But we cannot call flying a fear-object. It is only a situation in which crashing is a logical possibility. In fact, the plane almost always lands safely at the end of the flight.

So in the case of *rational fear*, where might fear-scenarios occur? The answer is in any situation where there is clear risk. The marine in active service will see the battle as a fear-scenario. For a woman in a deteriorating marriage relationship, the fear-scenario may be that her husband will get involved with another woman. In both cases, the fear-scenario is clearly distinguished from the fear-object. The precise object of the marine's fear is the possibility of death, injury, pain, or the loss of companions. For the woman, it is the total breakdown of her marriage.

Wild Wood fear and Big Bad Wolf fear

In both of the examples I've just given, the fear is rational. In both, there is an object and a context to the fear. But if you look more closely at what the two people are actually scared of (the fear-objects) you will see a difference.

The marine's fear is largely impersonal. He looks into the future and sees there a "thing," or series of "things," that may happen to him. If he is wounded in action, it will be another person who has pulled the trigger or thrown the grenade. But the two men will not know one another. Their relationship will be defined by their allegiance to their respective sides in the conflict.

Conversely, the woman's fear is largely personal. It is one person in particular to whom she is married. A soldier can be shot by anyone, but a wife can be betrayed only by her husband. What she fears, therefore, is not the experience of betrayal in the abstract, but the jarring of an important relationship by the action of the other party. Where the marine fears violation, the woman fears rejection.

I give these two types of fear-objects special names: *Wild Wood fear* and *Big Bad Wolf fear*.

In Kenneth Grahame's *Wind in the Willows*, the Wild Wood is the place nobody goes. Except the Mole, the bumbling hero of the book, on whom the warnings of the other animals are totally lost until, one day, he ventures in:

> The pattering increased till it sounded like sudden hail on the dry-leaf carpet spread around him. The whole wood seemed running now, running hard, hunting, chasing, closing in round something or—somebody? In panic, he began to run too, aimlessly, he knew not whither. He ran up against things, he fell over things and into things, he darted under things and dodged round things. At last he took refuge in the deep dark hollow of an old beech tree, which offered shelter, concealment— perhaps even safety, but who could tell? Anyhow, he was too tired to run any further, and could only snuggle down into the dry leaves which had drifted into the hollow and hope he was safe for the time. And as he lay there panting and trembling, and listened to the whistlings and the patterings outside, he knew it at last, in all its fullness, that dread thing which other little dwellers in field and hedgerow had encountered here, and known as their darkest moment—that thing which the Rat had

vainly tried to shield him from—the Terror of the
Wild Wood!

The quote gives a flavor of the terror of the Wild Wood. It's a
terror familiar to us all, a sense of foreboding and threat, an
awful feeling that something terrible is just about to happen
to us. The Wild Wood is thus a good metaphor for all those
fears that revolve around the anticipation of disaster. Anyone
who expects that something unpleasant is going to befall him
is suffering from a *Wild Wood fear*. At some point in the future,
he feels, some specific event is going to change his life un-
alterably for the worse.

My fear of becoming a target for terrorists is a *Wild Wood
fear*.

Another common example is the fear many elderly persons
have of falling. The danger is real—elderly folk who are frail
do sometimes fall and injure themselves, and sometimes
even die because they cannot reach a phone to call an ambu-
lance. Falling is thus a *rational Wild Wood fear*. So is the possibility of domestic violence for a woman whose husband is
drunk and aggressive, and the threat of persecution for the
Christian believer who is living under an oppressive regime.

Seeing some disaster in store for you is obviously a strong
motive for trying to avoid it. And this gives *Wild Wood fear* an
important application as a deterrent to crime—a useful way of
exacting obedience from persons not inclined to give it. The
fear-object is punishment: in theory, the fear of what will
happen to him if he is caught deters the wrongdoer from
committing a criminal act. Whether or not it does so in practice is a moot point, for children still disobey after threats of a
spanking, just as drug smugglers will risk the death sentence
to run heroin. They are winning over their fear, but wrongly,
because fear used as a deterrent protects society from damage
in much the same way as fear of injury protects the individual
from damage. A country with no fear of the law would
quickly destroy itself.

In a way, all fears have at their heart the "anticipation of
future disaster." But there is one group in which the disaster

is of a specially personal type, and I have called these *Big Bad Wolf fears*.

Big Bad Wolf fear always occurs within the victim's social circle. It may focus on his wife, parents, children, employer, employees, colleagues, or members of his church. The common feature is the breaking of existing relationships, such that he suffers a measure of rejection. Often it exists alongside other emotions, as when a child feels guilty over some misdemeanor and fears rejection by his parents if they find out. As the story of the Big Bad Wolf suggests, rejection can take an uncomfortably tangible form. The three pigs may have suffered a breakdown in relationship with the wolf, but he also threatened to huff and puff and blow their house down. Real-life examples aren't hard to find either. Domestic violence is rejection written in the language of physical pain. The loss of employment brings rejection, not in an abstract or emotional sense, but in the form of financial hardship.

Let's recap.

We have said that the first factor affecting the intensity of fear is the level of danger, and that as long as it is in proportion to the danger we face our fear is rational. We have seen how examples of *rational fear* demonstrate the difference between the fear-object (what we're really scared of) and the fear-scenario (the situation in which those fears may be realized). We have also seen how fear can be classed as *Big Bad Wolf fear* or *Wild Wood fear*, depending on whether the fear-object is personal or impersonal.

It is an enormous help to begin your victory over fear with a careful analysis of the enemy. I recommend that you take a while now to think about your fear. Can you distinguish the real fear-object? What are some of the fear-scenarios that haunt you? Most important, can you honestly say that your fear is *rational fear*, that it is proportional to the danger that inspires it? If you can, then your fear is legitimate. Though you dislike it, it is not an enemy—the fear is helping you by turning your attention to danger.

And if your fear isn't *rational fear*? Read on!

4

The Second Degree—
Exaggerated Fear

We have seen how the intensity of fear, "how scared we feel," depends on the level of danger. But that is not the only factor it depends on.

In the last chapter I talked about my fear of terrorism. I justified it as a *rational fear* because, first, the danger is real, and second, my response to the danger is proportional to its size. Consequently I am satisifed that my fear is legitimate. I am not overreacting to the danger by hiring a crowd of bodyguards and a bulletproof automobile. Nor am I treating it too lightly by failing to take sensible precautions for my safety.

Now all of this relies on a mental faculty called *perception*. Because I see the danger in its proper perspective, I am able to respond to it rationally without squandering my money on unneeded security measures or leaving myself unprotected. I rely on correct perception. In our daily experience we are always relying on correct perception. Take visual perception as an example. When you drive, shave, write, or throw a ball, you assume that what you see is a true representation of reality. If your visual perception were wrong, you wouldn't survive. Have you ever tried drawing pictures while looking in a mirror? It's a constant effort just to make a line go in the right direction. You rely on correct visual perception to coordinate your movements.

In the same way, you rely on correct mental perception to control your fear. Without that right perception, fear comes out of the servant's quarters and sits down at the head of the table.

The rationality gap

Imagine you could measure levels of danger on a scale, as you can measure people's heights and mark them on a graph.

At the bottom of the scale would come trivial dangers like having injections, and at the top, serious dangers like being kidnapped or being attacked by a grizzly bear.

Now, imagine that for each danger, you could mark with a cross the level of real danger and the level of *perceived* danger. What would happen if you tried out a few of the fears we've looked at so far—the *rational fears*?

In each case, the two crosses would fall in the same place. The person facing a grizzly bear has both his crosses near the top of the scale, because he quite rightly perceives the danger as acute. On the other hand, the person going for a smallpox vaccination has them near the bottom of the scale; there is no risk of serious injury, and after a brief moment of pain it will all be over.

Because their fears are *rational*, the actual danger and the perceived danger are on a par.

But what happens if the man going for his vaccination is frightened of needles? In fact, he dislikes them so much he even considers playing hooky and not going to the doctor. Is the danger any greater for him than for the other people having the vaccination? Of course not. The difference lies in his perception of the danger. For him, the cross showing the level of perceived danger is placed far higher on the scale than the cross showing the real danger.

We might call the distance between the two crosses the *rationality gap.*

It shows the amount of distortion present in a person's view of reality. The wider the *rationality gap*, the greater the distortion, and the greater the fear. That's why perception is the second factor affecting "how scared we are." It doesn't take a high level of danger to make a person afraid—all that's required is that he perceives a high level of danger. You probably realized that when you were eight years old and told your kid sister there was spider on her back!

The *rationality gap* is what moves first degree fear into the second degree. *Rational fear* gives way to *exaggerated fear.*

I use the term exaggerated because there is still a logical connection between the fear and the fear-object. The man who is scared of needles is justifiably scared, because having an injection is seldom a pleasant experience. The problem is that his fear response is out of proportion to the danger. Fear at the prospect of pain or discomfort is normal and is part of the body's defense mechanism. But he doesn't need to be as scared as he is. In his fear, he is exaggerating the danger.

"Okay," you respond. "I see that. But this man who fears needles has almost nothing to be scared of. I, on the other hand, fear something that is really dangerous."

I agree. I have used that example for the sake of clarity. In fact, most people with *exaggerated fears* can point to a fear-object much more dangerous than a vaccination. But that the danger is real and frightening is precisely what gives exaggerated fear its power. The fact that it is also unlikely to happen and perhaps easily avoided doesn't reckon in the calculations of the one who fears it. As is often the case, fear arises out of ignorance, misinformation, inadequate understanding, and the sheer impossibility of working out the odds.

On top of which other factors combine to make the situation worse. A major one is the high monetary value of scare stories as copy for newspapers and TV. Shootings, ghastly murders, rapes, massacres, accidents, and epidemics can always be relied on to increase the circulation and boost the ratings, but selecting materials of this sort inevitably gives a falsified account of the world, pumping it directly into the living room of the reader and viewer. If a morning news program reports a shooting in New York, feelings of fear associated with extreme violence are produced around thousands of breakfast tables in the rural Midwest. Are those people going to get shot themselves that day? The odds are less than one in a million. Yet they feel a twinge of fear. They feel another twinge when a report comes in about threats made to American travelers by terrorist organizations.

All of these matters are legitimate objects of fear. My point is simply that our culture tends to magnify them, making it easier to develop *exaggerated fear*.

The man whose perception is true will know that the threat posed to his personal safety is negligible. Nobody in his town has been shot for a hundred years. As for terrorism, he knows that in the particular countries he plans on visiting, he is unlikely to be a target.

Contrast that with the man who has exaggerated fear. Hearing about the shooting, he goes out and buys a handgun ("just in case") and for good measure keeps a loaded rifle under the stairs. And he certainly won't leave the country. Forget that long-promised trip to Europe he was going to take his wife on this year. They will go to Florida instead.

What I'm talking about here is one of the big problems of fear—that is, the power it has to control us. I'll return to this important effect of fear in chapter 7. For now, let's look in more detail at some of the common objects of *exaggerated fear*.

A short checklist of scares

1. *Illness—violation of the body*. Sickness and incapacitation are major fear-objects. Nobody likes to think that he might suffer a stroke, go blind, become chairbound or require a colostomy. Illness reduces the quality of life. Consequently a healthy person often harbors a fear of falling ill, and an ill person—especially if he has a progressive disease like cancer, multiple sclerosis, or AIDS—fears the worsening of his condition.

As a fear-object, illness comes in numerous forms. For the cancer patient, the object is narrowed to that one disease, and narrowed even further to the various pains, discomforts, and indignities to which he, as an individual, may be subjected by that particular cancer. At that stage his fear is likely to be rational. He knows more or less what is in store for him. The danger is real. And sometimes this very proximity to danger helps him to face up to it and win over fear.

Ironically, *exaggerated fear* of illness is more common among the healthy. The mother of a preacher friend of mine, a lovely and compassionate woman, suffered from the time of young motherhood the fear that she would die from cancer. When she did finally die (in her mid-70's) it was of a heart attack. She spent 40 years fearing the wrong ailment. But even if she had feared heart attacks for all that time, would it have done her any good? I doubt it!

Like all fear-objects, the fear of illness frequently comes packaged in a fear-scenario. The classic modern example is that of contact with an AIDS patient. But in general, the fear-scenario will be any situation where the fearing person thinks infection can be passed on or injury sustained (injury, in this case, can include medical treatment—especially if it is carried out by a dentist!). He may even fear certain places not for the perceived threat of illness, but simply because they remind him of it. Consequently he may be uncomfortable at having to visit a sick friend in the hospital.

A special category of illness (in the wider sense of violation of the body) is assault, an act of violence against the individual deliberately carried out by others. Rape belongs to this group; so, too, do mugging, torture, and crowd violence. The traumatic nature of all these experiences makes them objects of intense fear, the more so if a person has already been subjected to them once. Such a person will probably have vivid fear-scenarios. A woman who has been raped, for instance, may fear darkness, seclusion, or men. Clearly this fear has a rational basis. For a woman whose work takes her into situations of high risk, the fear of rape is a *rational fear*. But that very fact fosters an *exaggerated fear* of rape in women who are really not at risk.

It is possible to have the fear of assault vicariously—that is, not for yourself, but for someone you love. A young friend of mine who got married recently said to me, "The Lord will probably get even with me by giving me daughters. He knows how terrified I'll be when they get old enough to go out with young men. I know how I behaved in my teens, and it'll be torture thinking that these young men might be behaving in the same way!" His smile was too thin to hide the depth of meaning behind the remark. *Exaggerated fear* was already doing a number on him.

2. *Impoverishment—violation of finances.* By impoverishment I do not necessarily mean bankruptcy. The fear of impoverishment comes to the blue collar worker as an anxiety over

making ends meet, just as it comes to the New York financier when his stock crashes. As with illness, the fear-scenarios are many and varied. For some, the loss of employment or the calling in of a loan would be a fear-scenario. For others, it might be the unexpected addition of a family member, extra heating bills, or an event such as burglary. In personal finance, more than any other area, a person's thoughts are ruled by the question, "What would happen if . . . ?"

I am no psychologist, and I have not read any studies on the comparative response of men and women to financial stress. But after years of extensive contacts in the business world, I have come to the strange conclusion that while men are more prone to the vice of greed, it is in women that fear of poverty makes its greatest inroads into the mind.

Two years ago, I heard Dr. Gateri of Nairobi, an internationally respected psychiatrist, offer the opinion that the most pervasive fear in women is insecurity. My experience seems to bear this out. I have observed some women of great wealth suffering torments at the possibility that they would wind up in the poorhouse. Also, it is worthy of note that although the really big money in America is in the hands of women, it is men who do most of the big giving. I do not say this out of prejudice. Women are among the biggest donors to our organization. But as a group, they seem less willing to give large amounts than men, despite the fact that wealthy widows often have more money and more liquidity than their husbands had while they were alive. The reason? I am convinced it is *exaggerated fear*.

I am old enough to remember the Great Depression of the late '20's and '30's. During the intervening years I have watched men and women, who fear a repeat of those tragic times, take protective action that actually reduced their net worth. I know of some who to this very day keep their savings in cash. They refuse to trust banks or savings plans. Consequently in the last two decades high interest rates have stripped the value of their money by 60 percent.

3. *Bereavement—violation of relationships.* In a recent survey, *Psychology Today* (February, 1985) canvassed its readers to find

out what they were most afraid of. "More than 1,000 people responded," wrote Elizabeth Stark, "and chose death of a loved one overwhelmingly as their greatest fear. This was followed by serious illness. Financial worries and nuclear war tied for third."

Every normal person dreads the thought of losing a loving spouse, a devoted child, or a respected parent. But *exaggerated fear* lives in anticipation of bereavement. In my first church, I met a couple who had waited 14 years before God blessed them with a beautiful baby boy. But as soon as he was born they started to fear for his life. They stopped coming to church because they wanted to give every moment to the child. They were terrified by the thought that they might lose him. They would go to ridiculous measures to make sure he wouldn't catch cold, get his feet wet, or contract a disease. The regimen became oppressive. They smothered the child with doting concern.

Tragically, in spite of all their attentions, the lad died suddenly when he was only seven years old. A few months after the initial trauma of his death, the couple came back to church. They told me, "God, in His mercy, took the little boy to Himself—for the benefit of the child and to bring us back where God wanted us." They had been the victims of *exaggerated fear*.

As a footnote, I will add that bereavement doesn't only occur as a consequence of death. A woman whose husband travels in the Middle East may fear "bereavement" through kidnapping. Families living under totalitarian regimes are constantly afraid that a loved one may suddenly join the ranks of the "disappeared."

4. *Death—violation of life*. Death is the ultimate fear-object. It is a constituent of many other fear-objects (for instance, illness and old age), and a feature of many fear-scenarios (for instance, flying, war, and nuclear holocaust).

History records that those who were conscious at the time of death, and died outside the faith, have been tormented by it. The famous rationalist philosopher Thomas Hobbes died crying "Oh, it's a fearful leap into the dark!" Voltaire, seeing hallucinations of Christ at the foot of his deathbed, raised himself on one elbow and hissed, "Take that black man out of the room. Crush the wretch." Mariba could only beg for sedation.

It may seem that there is no cure for the fear of death. But I assure you there is. After living for 63 years, I tell you flatly that the Christian believer can win over the fear of death, from the moment he knows it is imminent.

One day a lady asked Dwight L. Moody if he was afraid to die. He told her he was. She remonstrated with him, saying she had heard him preach that God gave grace to die. He replied, "Madam, God does give grace to die. Right now He has given me grace to live. When the time comes for me to die, He will give me grace to die." Later Moody had a stroke and was rushed from Kansas City to his home in Massachusetts. Just before he died he said, "Earth is receding. Heaven is opening. This is my coronation day." God did give Moody grace to die as He had given him grace to live.

Even Dr. Daniel Drew, founder of Drew Theological Seminary, faced death triumphantly. His family had been called to his bedside. The doctors knew the end was near. Since he gave no sign of consciousness, one of his daughters asked, "Has he gone? Has he gone?" Her sister replied, "Feel his feet. Feel his feet. Nobody has ever died with warm feet."

At that Dr. Drew opened one eye and said, "Joan of Arc did." Then he died.

David said: "Whenever I am afraid, I will trust in You. . . . In God I have put my trust; I will not be afraid. What can man do to me?" (Psalm 56:3,11 NKJV). Trust in God overwhelms fear—even the fear of death. And if the fear of death can be beaten, you can win over any fear.

Bob Pierce, founder of World Vision, phoned me a few days before he died. He said, "John, I've told the doctors to remove the life support systems forever. So after I am taken off them, I will go into a coma and then pass over to be with the Lord. I want you to hook up your recorder because there are certain things I want to tell you before I go."

I still have in my possession the one and a half hours of recorded conversation with Bob Pierce I made on that day. Bob Pierce was in right standing with God, and anyone who has put his trust in God through faith in Jesus Christ's redemption on the cross of Calvary can face death unafraid. As a child of God on the threshold of death Bob Pierce knew, like Moody, that God gives grace to die.

You see, you can win over fear, even the fear of death.

5. *Rejection—breakdown of relationships.* The first four exaggerated fears on my checklist have been examples of *Wild Wood fear*, the fear of impersonal disaster. But it is equally possible to exaggerate the other sort of fear—*Big Bad Wolf fear*. Here the interest focuses not on the fear-object (rejection is the only fear-object in *Big Bad Wolf fear*) but on the ways in which it is expressed; in other words, on the fear-scenarios.

Rejection, in fact, lies at the root of a good many social fear-scenarios. Its most obvious guise is simple fear of criticism—having your opinions, ideals, actions or motives scorned by others. Fear of criticism can occur on its own, or be implicit in the fear of failure. Failure, in turn, plays a leading role in other common fears, such as fear of responsibility, fear of social interaction, and fear of taking examinations. All of these "high risk" situations the person with *exaggerated fear* will try hard to avoid. But others are more difficult. For example, old age, a complex fear-scenario, includes the threat of rejection through the weakening of your faculties and inability to form and maintain lifelong relationships. Finally, the fear of rejection is even present in guilt, the nightmare of what others would think of you if they ever found out about your past misdeeds.

I'll pick up on just one of those fear-scenarios, that of old age.

A very forthright Atlantan called Charlie Outlaw lived to the age of 86. He was a dynamic character. Almost single-handedly he brought Billy Sunday to Atlanta for a series of massive meetings. I doubt if there was a single major evangelical personality who came to Atlanta in the middle years of this century who did not know Charlie Outlaw. His apartment, shared with his wife Nell, an author, was guest quarters for people from all over the world.

But as Charlie Outlaw approached death he became a recluse. No pastor was allowed to visit him. Even his close friends were kept away. The reason was, he had developed an *exaggerated fear* that if people saw him in a weakened condition it would spoil the positive impressions that had built up about him over the years. He wished to die with dignity. But to do this, he had to grapple with the fear of old age—the fear of rejection.

5

The Third Degree—
Irrational Fear

I assert again: fear is fundamentally an asset. It recognizes danger and puts the body in a state of red alert until the danger is past, evaded, or overcome.

What I have called *exaggerated fear* is fear armed with binoculars. It sees big dangers a long way off, and small ones as though they were big. It overreacts, because the *rationality gap* separates the actual level of danger from the danger perceived by the fearing person. Naturally you can overreact a lot or a little. *Exaggerated fear* doesn't have to be intense. You need only one stamp to mail a letter. If you put on two, you are wasting stamps in the same way you would if you put on 15.

Exaggerated fear, however, does share one feature with *rational fear*. Both are able to distinguish a real danger and a false alarm. They are both logical.

But suppose a person is scared of worms—those pink, wriggly things you dig up in the garden. Believe it or not, the condition has a name. It's called *helminthophobia*. Now there is absolutely no way you can convince me that worms are dangerous. They won't sting you. They won't give you blisters. They don't carry infectious diseases. They won't poison you or suck your blood. They are totally harmless.

But try telling that to a helminthophobic! He won't listen. For him, that poor little helpless worm is a source of grave danger. As soon as he sees it he goes prickly all over and wants to get out of the way. He's so frightened he wouldn't dare tread on it. Why? I certainly have no idea. His perception isn't magnifying a danger, it's manufacturing one. He is seeing danger where there is really no danger at all. He is, in fact, suffering from fear in the third degree—*irrational fear*.

(In case you think I'm joking about the fear of worms, I'll tell you about a girl I know of who was terrified of them. She

61

lived in a basement flat in Vancouver, separated from the street by a long path. When it rained the path was covered with worms. She was so afraid of them that she would leave the house only if her boyfriend carried her!)

In practice, the distinction between *exaggerated fear* and *irrational fear* is a little hazy. There are some *exaggerated fears* where the danger, though real, is so small or so remote that the fear response is effectively irrational. These, together with the purely *irrational fears*, go to make up the class of anxieties the psychologists call "phobias."

Merriam-Webster's dictionary defines phobia as "an exaggerated, usually inexplicable and illogical fear of a particular object or class of objects." And phobia, according to *Business Week* (April 21, 1986), is on the increase. As a mental health problem it is second only to alcoholism. James O. Wilson, director of the Phobia Centers of the Southwest in Dallas, estimates that a single phobia, the fear of flying, is causing the airline industry to lose $1.5 billion a year.

What is the phobic afraid of? Sometimes nothing at all—or at least nothing he or anyone else can identify. But where the fear is focused, the list of fear-objects is virtually endless. At least three hundred phobias are common enough to have a specific name.

Mild phobias are widespread and, in most cases, fairly inoffensive. Serious phobias lead to all sorts of problems.

In 1972, the year of his reelection, Richard Nixon was being hailed by some as the brainiest president since James Madison. He had notched up some great achievements—détente with the Russians, a visit to Mao in China, the policy of floating the dollar. He was a "shoo-in" for a second term. George McGovern had about as much chance of winning that election as a snowflake has of surviving in the watery bosom of the Potomac. But Nixon developed an *irrational fear* of losing, and it drove him to one of the greatest political follies on record—Watergate. He didn't need to misuse the power of his office, but fear drove him to it. And today, though he is much admired as a speaker, writer, and political advisor, he is remembered as the first president to resign rather than face impeachment.

Phobia isn't only a scourge of politicians. My father's two brothers married sisters. In their late 80's they are still beautiful women. But when they were teenagers their mother had an *irrational fear* for their safety. So much so that every time a man came to read the gas or electricity meter, she would lock them in a back room. She did the same when the postman came. In fact, she did it when any man came. I believe it was only the fact that they married so young that saved them from emotional damage through their mother's fear.

I don't know what experiences lay behind that woman's behavior. But I know what lies behind the fear many Jewish people have of Germans. The Holocaust must go down as one of the foulest outrages in human history. And yet I'm not certain that the fear of Germans (Teutonophobia, to give its proper name) is a *rational fear* or even an *exaggerated fear*. There is no logical connection between the atrocities committed by the Third Reich and the individual German the Jew meets today, and only a tenuous one between Nazism and the modern nation of Germany. As with hospitals and illness, the fear is one of reminiscence.

That doesn't mean it's always easy to decide how dangerous a situation is. For instance, there was an orgy of killing in Indonesia following the failed Communist coup of September 30 - October 1, 1965. Estimates of the numbers slain range from 400,000 to more than two million. Among the dead were two family members of a friend of mine, innocents who had been killed in the panic. Their murder moved two local men to seek out the self-appointed executioners. When they found the murderers, they jumped them, beheaded them, and brought the severed heads to my friend in a burlap bag.

"We have avenged you," they said.

But my friend replied, "That is wrong. God says, 'Vengeance is mine. I will repay' " (Romans 12:19).

Why had the two men killed the executioners? Maybe it was a way of striking back at an impersonal evil. At any rate, the fear that they might be the next victims of those particular men was an *irrational fear.*

Irrational fear is the worst kind of fear. It has the widest *rationality gap,* and therefore gives the sufferer the most distorted view of reality. Of course, the fear-object may be trivial, or the fear mild. If you have a drastic phobia associated with lemon-scented geraniums or Scotland's blue-footed boobies, your lifestyle is unlikely to suffer! However, I think it is true that most phobias, and especially the common ones like agoraphobia (the fear of open spaces), are at best inconvenient, and at worst completely debilitating.

In God's power you can win over any irrational fear. There is absolutely no doubt about that. However, it is only fair to say here that you should not restrict your options. I trust you will find this book to be of vital assistance. But if your problem with fear arises from having a *rationality gap*—a faulty perception of the world—you may also benefit from consulting a reliable psychiatrist. I cannot, as a writer, necessarily pinpoint for you as an individual what we are turning to in the next chapter—the causes of fear.

6

What Does Your Fear Feed On?

Like pain, fear is a faculty we are born with. According to some psychologists there are some fears (noise, being alone, and falling) that babies have more or less from birth. But most fears are learned:

> Children pass through a sequence of fear stages. In the first year loud noises, strange or unexpected stimuli, and threats of bodily harm are mostly feared. Mother's departure becomes feared in the second year. The third year ushers in many fears, mostly auditory but also large objects, rain, wind, animals, and the dark (which often persists through to the sixth year). In the fourth year visual fears predominate, but in the fifth auditory fears again prevail. Five year olds show less fear, but the end of the sixth year may bring many fears—especially auditory stimuli and sleeping alone . . . (R.D. Kahoe)

Ideally all this ought to result in a balanced adult who experiences fear only in the first degree. In practice it does not. The God-given potential for entirely *rational fear* is corrupted to a greater or lesser degree in all of us. Our social environment exerts constant pressure on us, like a crosswind on an airplane, blowing us off course from first-degree fear into second-degree fear. The process begins in infancy and continues throughout life.

But what are the factors that contribute to it? It is important to our understanding of fear that we know not only what we are scared of, and in what way, but also what experiences give strength to that fear. So test out your fear in this chapter, and find out what it feeds on.

Childhood programming feeds fear.

Childhood programming is what ought to produce a mature and rational sense of fear. You may attribute the fact that it does not to one of several factors:

1. *The use of scare tactics.* One day when my son Johnny was three years old, a well-meaning relative who was trying to get him to eat said, "Now, Johnny, if you don't eat your food, a big bear will come and eat you."

Johnny's eyes opened wide. So did mine. I said to the relative, "Do you realize how you would respond if I could convince you that there was a real bear in the next room ready to come in here and eat you? Johnny believes what you tell him. I don't want you ever to make a statement like that to him again."

The relative had done it out of love and an innocent desire to help Johnny eat. It's an easy mistake to make. But I believe it is a mistake all the same.

A parent who blithely uses terror to get his way with children deprives them of the ability to look at danger rationally. He loads them up with pessimistic expectations and makes them targets for fear in later life.

2. *The role modeling of fear symptoms.* Children learn by imitation. If they see their parents exhibiting fear, they will exhibit fear. A woman wrote to an advice column asking why her three-year-old child had fits of trembling. She was, she added, an incredibly fearful person herself. That was the reason. Children of fearful parents are doubly exposed, for they lack the protection of the parents' confidence and suffer from the example of the parents' fear. So it is passed down from one generation to the next.

3. *The making of unrealistic demands.* Many parents are never satisfied. If a child gets a B at school, he is told he should have made an A. If he gets an A, then he should have made an A +. Consequently the message picked up by the child is not that achievement is rewarded, but that failure is criticized. Naturally he doesn't want to be criticized. The parents know that, and they are relying on it to motivate the child to higher

standards of attainment. But at the same time they are programming the child to fear.

No matter how innocent the motive, it is cruel to lay a guilt trip on children. My cousin asked his father one day, "Dad, why is it when you give your Christian testimony, you tell people what a bad boy you were before your conversion, but when you talk to us, you tell us what a good boy you were?"

Good question.

4. *The blows of disaster*. Some apparently random events can leave scars of fear on a child. I remember when I was nine hearing that the three-year-old daughter of some neighbors had moved too close to the warm heater one morning. When she turned around her little sweater caught the flame, and before the family could come on the scene to help her, she had been hopelessly burned. She died within 24 hours.

Her funeral was the first funeral I had attended. I shall never forget how the father wept. He wailed. He was convulsed with sobs. I had never heard a man cry audibly before, and it terrified me. Even now, 54 years later, I can feel the pain of that bereavement. Had it happened ten years later, it would not have been half so vivid. Because I was a child the impact was tremendous.

Media violence feeds fear

It seems curious to me that intelligent people who dismiss the effect of violence on the screen happily accept the logic of spending millions of dollars to advertise a product between programs. If a 30-second ad can persuade you to change your brand of wash powder, what is half an hour of violence going to do to you?

A few years ago, two beautiful young mothers were in a city park near my home. They worked at a bank and went to the park for lunch. One day two men jumped them, molested them, and tried to kill them. One of the women got away. The other, the daughter-in-law of a dear preacher friend of mine, was kicked so viciously that her heart literally exploded.

The attack was given wide coverage in the media. By chance, the reporting coincided with the showing of a TV film that portrayed a similar crime. The effect was staggering. I know people who, as a direct consequence of that event, installed burglar alarms, bought firearms, and put in wrought iron window bars, solid doors, and dead-bolt locks on their doors. Many of them also had their houses and grounds fitted with emergency lighting that could be flipped on at the turn of a single switch, illuminating the entire area.

An even better measure of the effect of media violence is the response of those who know America only through its television programs. Many of my friends in Asia are convinced that life in the United States is just as they see it on *Miami Vice*. They wouldn't dream of visiting me. When I tell them I have never seen a man shot, never seen a gun battle in my town, never even seen a person robbed, they stare at me in disbelief. They exemplify the point made to me by my colleague, Dr. Harold Keown, who has years of experience in psychology of communication studies, that aggressive and violent behavior shown on the media produces fear and anxiety in the viewer.

Pain feeds fear

"Beware of dogs" is one warning that always captures my attention. I got my first bite, courtesy of a neighbor's dog, when I was only four years old. I think the growl terrified me as much as the bite, though he certainly took some skin with him.

Some years later, cautious inquiries to another dog owner elicited reassurances. "Fido never bites anyone. He's just a good watch dog, but he won't attack." He did.

The last straw came several years ago when I returned from a trip overseas. My wife had phoned me while I was away to tell me she'd been given a beautiful little dog called Brownie. I'd forgotten all about Brownie until I arrived in Atlanta at two o'clock in the morning. Not wanting to cause a disturbance, I opened the door quietly and crept in. But before I could switch on the light there was an explosion of canine belligerence that sent my hair straight up. For the next ten minutes

I went at it with this beast, determined to end his miserable life as soon as I could get my hands on him. He was saved by my wife, who had been awakened by the noise and came in to break up the fight. One word from her and Brownie turned as nice as a bowl of peaches and cream.

To this day, I am terrified of strange dogs. I'm okay once I've been introduced to them—politely and officially. In fact, we've recently acquired another dog, indelicately named Pookie, who I am relieved to say shows every indication of liking me. But the fear remains. I tell my friends, "If you want me to visit you, chain up the livestock before I arrive!"

Far deeper and more pervasive than physical pain is emotional pain. For instance, I can think of one of America's most eligible Christian bachelors whose influence and effectiveness is limited because he will not trust any woman. His wife had so shattered his confidence by her wanton sexual behavior prior to finally leaving him, he felt he was the laughing stock of the city.

The physical pain of a dog bite cannot remotely approximate the soul and heart pain this man has endured. Unfortunately, he has not demonstrated the necessary maturity to face up to the fact that one errant woman does not represent all womanhood, one intolerable marriage does not represent all marriages, and one unconscionable rejection does not represent all female behavior.

He has allowed the continual replay of his pain to make him the hostage of an ever deepening fear.

Feelings of inadequacy feed fear

Moses is a perfect example of this. Read Exodus chapters 3 and 4, where God gives Moses his job interview for the leadership of Israel. A more diffident candidate you could not hope to meet. God tells him all the mighty victories in store for him, and all Moses does is look for excuses:

> Moses said unto the Lord, O my Lord, I am not eloquent, neither heretofore, nor since thou hast

spoken unto thy servant: but I am slow of speech,
and of a slow tongue (Exodus 4:10).

In other words, "Send somebody else!" Moses tried to
evade his calling because he felt inadequate. He dug in his
heels. In the end, God got angry with him and said, "Okay, if
you insist on working from behind the scenes, I'll get your
half brother Aaron to be your mouthpiece." I wonder if later
on Moses didn't regret letting his fears get the better of him.

It's no use measuring out your wheat by someone else's
bushel. You will come out depressed because their bushel
isn't the same size as yours. Don't compare yourself with
others all the time. Accept the fact that God will provide for
you the necessary adequacy to accomplish whatever He calls
you to do. This is His special provision to you to win over fear.

Ego defense feeds fear

It is also true the other way around—fear feeds ego defense. The two exist in symbiosis. Because a person is afraid of
losing his credibility he defends his ego by building up his
image with others. But the more he builds up his image, the
more insecure he gets.

I personally know some Christian celebrities who go to
unbelievable lengths to arrange testimonials on their own
behalf! Of course they launder the idea. The person who
actually fixes up the dinner with government, educational, or
business leaders probably ends up thinking the testimonial
was his own idea. But the sole purpose of the event is to build
up the ego of the man at the top of the organization—an
ordinary man who is trying to camouflage his ordinariness
by orchestrating the praise of others.

It reminds me of the man who felt so inadequate that he
asked to be paged at a convention so he would come to the
attention of the people he wished to impress.

A distorted concept of God feeds fear

Often I have been asked why God permits terrorism, futile
wars, torture of innocents, and so on. There is a phony logic at

work behind this question. The Bible says God is all-powerful and all-loving. For suffering to exist in the world He has made, therefore, implies either that He loves us but is helpless to prevent our suffering, or that He could prevent it if He wanted to but prefers to watch us suffer.

The logic is phony because it leaves out the doctrine of human sin. We don't have to fear that God's hands are tied. They are not. He is omnipotent. Nor do we have to fear that He laughs at our suffering. His love, like His power, is absolute. The weak link in the chain is the ability of the sinful world to receive that love. It is when we refuse to trust God, in the totality of His power and love, that we become subject to fear.

The only way God could impose peace on the world would be to robotize our wills and rob every human being of the power of choice. He has not chosen to do that. He has given every person a free will. If someone prostitutes that power of choice to unworthy ends, don't blame God. If someone comes into my home, lights up a cigar, and flips the ashes on the floor so that the curtains catch fire and the house burns down, I would be foolish to blame God for the destruction of my home; it was that careless fellow who flipped his cigar ashes on my floor.

It never ceases to amaze me how people who fight among themselves in their own homes somehow seem to think that there can be peace and serenity in a world made up of people just like them. As long as we enjoy the divine gift of free choice, we are also saddled with the responsibility of the results those choices bring about.

7

Fear Feeds on You!

In the end you are the prize entrée on the menu of fear.

Having a fear is like having a cancer. It is always there, hidden inside you, always sapping your strength and breaking your concentration. Even *rational fear* can be destructive in its effects. What is popularly called "shell shock," for instance, is really nothing of the kind. It is a form of mental breakdown resulting from the prolonged endurance of *rational fear*—a conflict, if you will, between a soldier's natural fear on the battlefield, and the sense of duty (or perhaps the fear of punishment for not performing it) that makes him stay there.

You cannot hide fear. Its destruction begins by feeding on you, and then moving into your social and physical environment. Let me illustrate.

There are many avowed evangelicals who profess a strong faith in the Bible. But scratch the surface a little, and you will uncover a strange paradox. While they believe in the Bible, they also harbor a perpetual fear that research in theology or the spade in archeology will one day uncover something to disprove the very Scriptures they profess to believe. The result? There is a setting in motion of precedents and policies that stifle legitimate scholarship.

Again, for nearly 20 years I tried, in every way I knew how, to get an appointment with a man whose behavior signaled the message that I had offended him. He would not answer my letters. So I went through intermediaries, some of his closest friends, in the hope of seeing him. All to no avail. Now the Bible says that if there is a problem between me and my brother, I must go and talk to him about it. But how can I do that if I cannot reach him? He is one of that growing number of Christian celebrity untouchables. Their phones are unlisted. They live in a compound behind a high wall or

73

in a remote area where normal access is impossible. When they move they are surrounded by a huge entourage and insulated from the real world by a coterie of assistants and bodyguards. To me that behavior spells one word—fear.

I was once asked on a television interview, "Dr. Haggai, after your extensive world travels, what is the most amazing observation you have made?"

"You mean in the United States or overseas?"

"In the United States."

"The most amazing observation is the prevailing insecurity of the average American."

"Did this surprise you?"

"It shocked me. I couldn't believe it."

I still cannot, and yet the years have only confirmed and reconfirmed the observation.

A child wants to go to a certain event. The mother has to call every other mother in the neighborhood before she can make up her mind. A family decides to go on a vacation, but they have to find the "in" place before they finalize their plans. If that colorful evangelist Cyclone Mac (Baxter F. McClendon) were still alive today, he would say, "They're all like baloney sausages, stuffed with the same thing and wrapped in the same cover. Bite one in California, and it tastes exactly like one bitten in New Jersey."

I was flying one night across the country. During the flight, while nearly everyone was asleep, I turned on my individual light to read my Bible. A young man across the aisle said, looking at the Bible, "Oh, reading from Jeremiah, are you?"

"Yes, are you a Christian?"

"I'm a Jew."

"Where is your native home?"

"Jerusalem. I was born, reared, and educated there."

"Where do you live now?"

"Dallas, Texas, where I serve as a professor at the University of Texas. Before that I taught at McMaster's University in Canada."

"Well, I guess that the adjustment to this hemisphere was made when you moved from Jerusalem to Canada, and the move from Canada to Dallas was probably an easy move, with virtually no change except the weather change."

"That's not true. The minute I crossed the Canadian border, the stress factor zoomed up at least a thousand percent."

"I can't believe that. Explain it to me."

"In the United States you brag on your individualism, but you demonstrate a herd instinct. I'll give you an illustration. In Canada, I drove a 1968 Chevrolet. Nobody seemed to be upset with that. I lived in a particular house in a particular section of town. In Dallas, while they'll not come out and say it, they communicate nonverbally that driving a 1968 Chevrolet when you are a man in my position is not acceptable, and they let you know in a hurry what type of home and what part of the city you need to live in and where your children ought to go to school. These people seem to be filled with fear that they are not going to be accepted."

I told him that I thought his judgment was somewhat harsh, but I've never forgotten that midnight conversation with the young Jewish professor from Dallas.

The lesson is transparently clear: *fear has the most insidious power over its victims.*

The ruins of fear

Illegitimate fear in general—*exaggerated* and *irrational*, *Wild Wood* and *Big Bad Wolf*—has a stunning list of destructive effects.

1. *Fear means lack of influence.* Imagine you're at a lecture, and the speaker gets up and says: "I don't know why they called me to speak on this subject. I'm really not qualified. There are scores of people who are more qualified than I am— in fact, many of them are in this room. I really don't want to waste your time, so if there's somebody else here who'd like to speak instead . . ."

Doesn't exactly inspire confidence, does it? Fear undermines personal dynamism. Instead of being a person who knows where he is going and emits an enthusiasm that motivates others, you perpetually apologize and thus decrease your influence in the group.

My brother Tom is one of the world's premier speakers to business and professional groups. He passed on to me an astute observation a couple of years ago. "When a speaker like Mr. So-and-So, who gets $5,000 for every speech he makes, comes to a group and tells them what a hectic schedule he has kept and how many miles he has traveled and how little sleep he has had, he really does himself a disservice. The people sponsoring him did not scrape up the money for the honorarium in order to hear about his fatigue. They came to hear his oration and receive benefit from his insights. Why would he, one of the most accomplished speakers in the world, resort to currying sympathy from the audience?"

Tom didn't need to elaborate. The man was afraid. He wanted to neutralize his audience so they would be favorably disposed to him.

2. *Fear means truant thoughts.* Fear divides the mind much like worry and keeps the fearing person from focused thinking. Consequently he has little control over his thoughts. They range freely across the possibilities of disaster and tend to create a sense of panic and crisis that reinforces fear.

A friend of mine who works with the elderly in Scotland knows a couple with an *irrational fear* of mice. They think that if a mouse gets under their floorboards, it will ceratinly get into the roof, and once it's in the roof, it will certainly chew through the power cables and cause a short circuit and begin a fire. Truant thoughts have inflated the fear of mice into a fear of death.

The apostle Paul did not allow fear to confuse his thinking. He was absolutely committed to the spreading of the gospel, and while he was a man of mortal mean and mold, he could say of the hindrances he faced, "None of these things moves me." He directed his thoughts to good and edifying subjects. And he advised the Philippians to do the same:

> Finally, brethen, whatever things are true, whatever things are noble, whatever things are just,

whatever things are pure, whatever things are of good report, if there is any virtue and if there is anything praiseworthy—meditate on these things. (Philippians 4:8 NKJV).

Truant thoughts do not deal with love, truth, justice, or anything else that is positive. They entertain fantasies of harm—premature death, the child's flunking out of school, the betrayal of friends, or the leaving or death of a spouse.

What is the answer to truant thoughts? There is only one: Christocentricity—putting Christ where He ought to be, at the center of your life. Christ requires thoughts, as well as actions, that honor Him. So every thought should be brought into captivity to the obedience of Christ (see 2 Corinthians 10:5).

I remember accompanying the venerable Dr. Robert G. Lee, my favorite role model as a pastor, back to his study after a meeting. During the business session of that meeting he had burst out, "If you people who are always criticizing me knew how little your criticism meant, you would save your breath."

Because Dr. Lee loved me, he allowed me certain liberties, so I said to him rather wistfully, "Dr. Lee, I wish I could come to the place where criticism of other people did not affect me adversely."

He looked at me and said, "Oh, John, when I think of the hours I've wasted in the course of my life fretting about the criticisms of others—hours I could have utilized writing or visiting or memorizing—it would depress me if I gave much time to it."

That he didn't give much time to brooding over criticism was a measure of his power over fear.

3. *Fear means boredom.* Boredom is the side effect of implementing a no-risk policy in your lifestyle.

The fearful person often refuses to mix socially because he fears his looks are not adequate, his conversation is dull, his opinons are shallow. The fears may be groundless at first. But just like a car engine deteriorates through lack of use, so does a person's ability to socialize, and he will often get to the stage where experience corroborates his suspicions. He withdraws, not wanting to be hurt. But on the other hand, he doesn't want to live alone. He has more potential than his fear will allow him to express. As a result he suffers boredom.

4. *Fear means struggle.* Men who are short of stature know how painful it can be to lack those few vital inches. As a child, it's humiliating to be on the end of the group in every class picture, to be shorter even than the girls. It can affect your health! I am informed by our director of administration, Lieutenant Colonel (retired) Norman Vaughn, that studies done at West Point show short men to have more heart attacks, more health problems, and more often more difficulty in getting along with their peers. In fact, there is an Arabic proverb that runs, "Be careful of the man who is too close to the ground."

Many short men have overcome the fears associated with their height. Alexander the Great, Napoleon, and John Wesley were all only five feet tall. More often, though, the fear produces a constant struggle to compensate. For example, a short boy at school will often try to excel at sports, not through love for a particular sport, but in an effort to win the approval of his fellows and overcome the fear of his short stature.

A less rational form of the same mechanism is what the psychologists call obsessional neurosis. Here a fearing person adopts an obsessive habit that he feels will keep danger at bay. There is no logical basis for his choice. If I try to touch wood everytime I express a hope, or try not to walk on the cracks between paving stones, the action will do nothing to avert danger. More likely, it will only result in my fear being intensified when I forget to do it.

5. *Fear means financial errors.* It was fear that led to the 1929 Wall Street crash. People were buying stocks on a 90 percent margin. If the stock was $100, they would put up $10 and borrow $90. When the stock dropped to $50, they were required to put up another $40, which they didn't have. They were making financially disastrous decisions. Why? For fear of losing out on potential wealth.

Contrast that with the conduct of a businessman who came to America from Europe in the year of the crash. I know the story well because I know his son. This man brought all of his savings to the United States to set up business here. America was his chief market, and President Hoover had put 100 percent duty on the merchandise the business man was making. He was practically forced to move from his native Germany to America if his business were to remain viable.

When he got here, this German businessman found that nearly everyone he met told him the same thing: "Put your money in the market. You can make millions." But he resisted. He did not give in to the fear of losing out on a quick kill, the fear of being unable to compete with others who would certainly outstrip his economic growth if the market continued to rise. Of course, it didn't. The market crashed. In a matter of months, the men who had urged him to play the market had lost everything. Some were reduced to peddling apples and pencils on the street. Others committed suicide. He was sitting on a pile of cash.

Shortly after the crash, this German businessman was able to buy a 100,000-square-foot factory in Massachusetts for $25,000 cash. It was the start of one of the most incredible success stories in the annals of American industry. Today the company he founded is one of the most prestigious on the "Big Board"—the New York Stock Exchange.

6. *Fear means time dissipation.* I read yesterday that journalists don't have mental blocks because they are always working toward a deadline.

A deadline is a lifeline. Perfectionism can be unrealistic—after all, nobody really achieves full efficiency at work. It's better to do all your work at 96 percent of your potential than it is to do only half of it at 98 percent. In writing, certainly, the art lies in plunging in and not standing on the side waiting for the pool to be perfectly still so you can see the bottom. The British novelist John Braine, who wrote *Room at the Top*, advocated that you get at least 60,000 words down on paper before you begin to exercise your critical faculties.

Why is it so hard to push ahead and get things done? Probably because action means forging into the unknown, abandoning the familiar territory of what you have done before and trying your hand at something new. Fear procrastinates. And once it is in control, fear will supply you with a thousand good reasons for procrastinating.

Take the case of that strange creature, the professional student. He never moves more than five miles from the campus. He gets his degrees, goes on to postdoctoral studies, locks himself firmly in the ivory tower of academia. He never comes in contact with the real world. He is secure in an intellectual environment where no demands are made of him beyond the exercise of his own narrow expertise. He seems to be productively employed, but he's not. He is dissipating time in the illusion of productivity because he is afraid to take a risk and leave the academic nest. Fear chews away at his life.

7. *Fear means conformity.* One day a man approached my evangelist friend, Eddie Lieberman, who was holding a meeting in a southern town. The man had a large Bible under his arm and a broad grin on his face. He pumped Eddie's hand.

"I want you to know, hallelujah, bless God, amen, that we sure love the Lord, and hallelujah, amen, and blessed be God, we are walking in the light and in the power of the Spirit!"

Eddie smiled, said "God bless you," and walked on.

Next day another man, with a similar Bible and similar grin, approached him and gave him the same line. This time Eddie interrupted. "I know where you're from."

"Yes? Where?"

Eddie mentioned the group, whereupon the man said, "Oh, I guess you could tell us because we are all so different."

"No, the truth is, you're all exactly the same."

I've come across the same phenomenon myself. Some years ago, I met some friends who expressed their Christian faith in a totally unique vocabulary of super-saint trigger words. I wanted to be gracious, but I knew that if the average person heard them, he would think they were on an outing from the insane asylum. I determined not to play ball, and next time I met one of them on the street I asked him how he was.

"Isn't Jesus precious?" he replied.

I nodded. "I know how Jesus is. How are you?"

That floored him.

I know it says in Scripture that we are not to be of this world. But it also says we have to be in it. People will recognize the language of Zion without us festooning it in catchphrases. As ambassadors of God, it is our duty to pay due regard not only to the laws and customs of the kingdom of heaven but also to the culture of the people to whom we have been sent. The use of religious jargon is a sign of fear—a way of reinforcing the point that we are members of a certain in-group. This doesn't mean that we ought to adopt the jargon of the world through fear of being seen as oddballs. Fear should not make us conformists to any mere cultural trait, Christian or otherwise.

8. *Fear means godlessness*. Fear leads to godlessness because it opposes faith. I'll look at this further in a later chapter. But note how in the story of the storm, found in Mark 4:35-41, the disciples were forced into godlessness through their fear.

Terrified by the sudden storm, they woke Jesus, who had gone to sleep in the bottom of the boat. "Master, save us!" they cried. "We perish!" Jesus arose and rebuked the wind, and the sea became as calm as a millpond. "Why were you so fearful?" he asked them.

They could have replied, "Are you kidding? In all our years at sea we've never seen a storm like that, and you call us fearful?" They didn't, probably because they realized that being in the presence of Jesus turned their old assumptions upside down. Jesus had said when they left the shore, "Let's go to the other side," not, "Let's go out in the middle of the lake and drown." Why had they not believed that when the storm came up? Simply through fear.

9. *Fear means health problems*. Fear is closely related to worry, and tends to produce the same physical effects. Prolonged

illegitimate fear puts the body under a strain that is only meant to be endured in short bursts, for engagement with immediate danger. Among other things, fear causes tension in the muscles, restriction of the cardiovascular system, pressure in the head, and intestinal problems like duodenal ulcers.

10. *Fear means premature death.* The accumulation of stress cannot help but wear down the body and shorten life. Consequently I class the toleration of fear, when the fearing person knows he can do something about it, as a socially acceptable form of suicide, slower but just as effective as blowing your brains out with a gun or taking an overdose.

Fear kills in other ways. It kills in the culture of the Australian aborigines through "pointing the bone," a ritual in which psychosomatic death, induced by fear, follows in a person who has been condemned by the witch doctor. It kills in the West through a person's unwillingness to seek medical treatment. My Uncle Bill died at 49 from a strangulated hernia because he feared having surgery. Another man, whose nephew is a dear friend, died of a heart attack because he was so surprised to find, having convinced himself and everyone else that surgery was going to kill him, that he had come through alive!

Fleeing from the Big Bad Wolf

In addition to the complications of fear I've listed above, there is a wide range of specifically social difficulties that arise from *Big Bad Wolf fears*. To live in constant fear of rejection by others is to cripple yourself socially. It affects your work, your marriage, your leisure time and casual contacts. You live, like pigs in the story, in dread of the Big Bad Wolf.

If you have a fear founded on rejection, I suspect you will have trouble with the following.

1. *Forming relationships.* Making friends with someone involves risk. Starting a romantic relationship involves even greater risk. The fearful person will need a lot of persuading to begin a venture like that. And once he has begun, fear will

tend to make him too sensitive. Fear comes home from a party and replays every word and every nuance, interrogating them for signs of indiscretion. It is afraid of giving offense and upset at receiving it. It is also prone to wild flights of imagination.

I have seen long-standing friendships wrecked because one party, like Shakespeare's Othello, became possessed of jealous fears. I know of a man whose neighbor moved across the country after living for years in the same town. When the neighbor didn't write, his friend felt rejected and wrote a nasty letter, thus beginning an exchange of abusive correspondence which ruptured the friendship. In fact, the reason for the neighbor's silence was his involvement in an automobile accident. He had been on the critical list for months.

2. *Accepting responsibility*. The fearful person never wants to be in the place where the buck stops. If he is going to make a mistake, he would rather do it in private. So to avoid criticism he cancels meetings, misses deadlines, sidesteps personnel problems, and delays, delays, delays.

Some women avoid responsibility in the home, too. They spend their days munching on potato chips and watching soap operas. They don't plan in advance. Their shopping is haphazard. They don't keep their checkbooks reconciled or retain receipts for income tax purposes. They oversleep, leaving their children to shift for themselves in getting ready for school. The house usually looks like the last visitor was a tornado.

3. *Taking criticism*. The fearful person is rarely willing to learn from criticism. I know some writers who are capable of reaching the best-seller list, but who will not take criticism from editors. As a result they lose out and thousands are deprived of their valuable insights.

One of the most gifted men I've ever known lost his health and his company through repeated outbursts of fear-inspired temper. He saw behind every critical comment the danger of his losing control. Ironically, it was this very fear that wrested control of his multinational organization from him. His trumpcard in policy arguments was the threat to resign. He played it whenever he wanted to get his own way, and it never failed. Never, that is, until he played it once too often. After one of his raging scenes, culminating in a threat of resignation, a board member quietly moved to accept his resignation "with regrets."

The vote was unanimous.

4. *Facing confrontation.* No great goal was ever achieved without bringing the protagonist into confrontation with his opponents.

It's easy to write letters, easy to make others do the dirty work, easy to spiel off from behind a podium. But fear will not willingly confront another person and argue out differences. Paul wrote to the Galatians about how he had had to shame Peter into confronting the Judaizers. Peter, who had been the first Christian to take the gospel to the Gentiles, later lost the courage to do it. He tried to fudge the issue by appeasing them. Fear had gained the upper hand.

5. *Braving failure.* I was one of four boys in my family. One died in infancy. The youngest of the survivors, Tom, was ordained a minister, as I was. This put a lot of pressure on Ted. People would make remarks to him. "You say your father is a minister, and your two brothers are ministers?"

"Yes, they are."

"Isn't it interesting that you should not have gone into the ministry?"

Loaded question! How would you have answered it without coming across as defensive? I recoiled at hearing him baited like that and sometimes cut in to defend him. "God knows that while there are some men outside the ministry who should be in it, there are many more in it who should never have gotten there!"

Ted was 16 months my junior. I made good grades at school; Ted horsed around. He graduated only by the grace of the principal. Yet he went on to become a celebrated electrical engineer and led the project that put the SYNCOM satellite into space. I didn't know until his funeral that much of the

AWAC surveillance system was the product of Ted's scientific genius. How easily all that could have been lost had Ted given in to his fears of failure. I know he had them. But he had the strength not just to overcome his failures at school, but to risk further failure by defying the opinions of others and being his own man, doing what he knew was right for him.

For me, Ted stands out as a shining example of a man who won over fear. If you want to follow him, turn to the next section.

Part 3

How To Win Over Fear

8

Fear—And Fear Not

I want to make one point clear before I go any further.

Many of the so-called solutions to fear are psychological—they are ways of training your mind not to go overboard on the fear response, or of learning to tolerate an irrational fear stimulus (like worms) without breaking out in a cold sweat. These methods have their place; I do not disparage them. In fact, I recommend some of them in this book. But you must understand that they are not a complete answer. There is only one place where total freedom from fear can be found, because it is in that one place alone that the deepest causes of fear are healed. The place is the person of God.

The old fear of God

Winning over fear—and I mean really *winning*, not just learning to live with it—begins, paradoxically, with fearing in the right way.

Look at this passage from the Gospel of Matthew:

> Fear not them which kill the body, but are not able to kill the soul: but rather fear him which is able to destroy both soul and body in hell.
>
> Are not two sparrows sold for a farthing? And one of them shall not fall on the ground without your Father. But the very hairs of your head are all numbered. Fear ye not therefore, ye are of more value than many sparrows (Matthew 10:28-31).

Jesus has been talking to the disciples about persecution. Don't be under any illusions, He says. Follow Me, and you will be like sheep in a wolf pack. You will be tried and scourged. You will be turned into refugees. You will be hated so much that even members of your own family will betray you.

For the full story, read through Matthew 10:16-27. It's not comfortable reading, is it? Jesus lists experiences, the prospect of which would scare any normal person to death. And then, suddenly, He puts the warning in context: "fear not them which kill the body . . . but rather fear him which is able to destroy both soul and body in hell. . . ." In other words, put your fears in the right order of priority. The torturer, the accuser, and the Judas are all legitimate fear-objects, but they are not to be feared as God is.

The Bible is adamant in its teaching that fallen man's first and most appropriate response to God is fear. It was with good reason that Adam hid in the bushes and said "I was afraid." He had disobeyed God's explicit command, and so has everyone else since. Adam enjoyed a unique privilege, however, inasmuch as his judgment was immediate. He had just enough time to sew a few fig leaves together before he heard God come out for His evening stroll in the garden. Consequently, Adam had the opportunity neither to reconcile himself to his guilt, nor to anesthetize his conscience and forget what had happened.

The same cannot be said of Adam's descendants. What makes much human sin so reprehensible is the shamelessness with which it is committed. Every sinner, perhaps, thinks twice when he reaches the gates of death, but in the meantime, on the far-roaming highways of life, he strides on in the happy delusion that his journey will never end and that he will not be held to account for his actions on the way:

> As it is written, there is none righteous, no, not one: There is none that understandeth, there is none that seeketh after God. . . .the way of peace they have not known: there is no fear of God before their eyes (Romans 3:10,11,17,18).

Brazen ignorance of the fear of God can be traced in a direct line from Cain's murder of his brother in Genesis 4 to the atrocities you saw reported on the news last night. The man with no fear of God makes himself an enemy of God, and the place of enmity with God is fertile ground for every other sort of fear: the fear of loss that results in fratricide, and the fear of embarrassment at the ballot box that results in rigged elections and military oppression.

But if the refusal to fear God is the gateway to folly, the converse is also true: that, as the writer of Proverbs puts it, "The fear of the Lord is the beginning of knowledge" (Proverbs 1:7). It is the beginning of many other blessings, too: longevity (10:27), confidence (14:26), life (14:27), and satisfaction (23:17). The Wisdom writers of the Old Testament urge on us again and again the magnitude of God's blessing to those who fear Him:

> He will bless them that fear the Lord, both small and great (Psalm 115:13).

> The Lord taketh pleasure in them that fear him, in those that hope in his mercy (Psalm 147:11).

Mary picks up the same theme in the New Testament, when she says in the presence of Elizabeth, mother of John the Baptist:

> He that is mighty hath done to me great things; and holy is his name. And his mercy is on them that fear him from generation to generation (Luke 1:49,50).

What does it mean, then, to fear God?

Practically the only New Testament Greek term for "fear" is used here by Mary, and also by Jesus in Matthew 10. It is a strong word, meaning literally "to be terrified of," which at first makes the contexts of its use a little strange. Mary links fear with mercy; and Jesus, advocating the fear—the terror—of God, goes on to emphasize His fatherly care.

An impossible combination?

Not quite. You see, man's relationship with God must begin with profound fear because, like Adam, we have disobeyed him. You, I, and everybody else have at some time been, as it were, hiding in the undergrowth, desperately trying to cover ourselves with fig leaves. We are guilty, and we know it. For some people, this guilt, this sense of utter unworthiness, lingers on to undermine every area of life. But it ought not. Guilt is the right place to start, but the wrong place to stay.

There is a famous passage written by John in one of his epistles:

> My little children, these things I write to you that you may not sin. And if anyone sins, we have an Advocate with the Father, Jesus Christ the righteous. And He Himself is the propitiation for our sins, not for ours only but also for the whole world (1 John 2:1,2 NKJV).

John is not writing to just anybody. He is addressing a readership of Christians, and it is Christians—those who have let guilt lead them to repentance and faith in Jesus Christ—for whom the propitiation, the sacrifice, is effective. I remember Dr. Chandu Ray expressing it perfectly when he lifted his voice and said of Jesus, "He is the annulment of our guilt."

To have your guilt "annulled" is to enjoy a totally new status before God. That status is unaffected by fresh guilt. It goes without saying that one of the first things any of us do after we are converted is sin. Becoming Christians doesn't make us immune to that. But sin cannot turn us back into nonbelievers. When we confess our sins, we do so not in order to secure our status, but because that status has already been secured. It is like the child apologizing to the parent, not in order to become a child, but because he is already a child and does not want to grieve the parent.

True Christianity could thus be defined as "the religion of the clean conscience." This is made possible through the fear—the terror—of God. Fear produces repentance, and repentance produces the blessings of a new status before God—a new status which I hope by now you have received.

But there is something else, too.

The new fear of God

When the new status is bestowed, the old sin-inspired terror of God should be transformed into a new sort of fear—fear in the sense meant by the Wisdom writers of the Old Testament. It has two elements.

1. *Fearing God means holding Him in awe and respect.* The most common word for "fear" used by God's people in the Old Testament would not describe the experience you have while watching a horror movie. Rather, it is the fear you might feel the first time you see the Grand Canyon, or are ushered into the Oval Office to speak to the president of the United States. You might call it "reverence."

Reverence shares with what I've called the "old fear of God," and with other fears in general, a sense of being overwhelmed. What scares us about a fear-object, be it a righteous God or a grizzly bear, is the gut-feeling that we are vulnerable in the presence of someone or something greater and more powerful than we are. Reverence balances that feeling with the assurance of safety. The man at the Grand Canyon is awed by its immensity, but at the same time he feels as though he belongs, as though he has a right to be there. The man about to shake hands with the president knows that he is accorded the rights and privileges of a citizen, though his heart is in his mouth.

Still, reverence gives neither man permission to take liberties. Only a churl would turn his nose up at natural beauty; and if the man visiting the White House took advantage of the occasion to give offense, he would receive short shrift from the security staff.

This fine balance of safety and respect, privilege and responsibility, lies at the heart of the "new fear of God." It causes Paul to write to Ephesians about "submitting yourselves one to another in the fear of God" (Ephesians 5:21); and to the Philippians to "work out your own salvation with fear and trembling" (Philippians 2:12). In both passages the sense of the word fear is "reverence." Peter sums it up neatly in his first epistle:

> As he which hath called you is holy, so be ye holy in all manner of conversation; because it is written, Be ye holy; for I am holy. And if ye call on the Father, who without respect of persons judgeth according to every man's work, pass the time of your sojourning here in fear (I Peter 1:15-17).

2. *Fearing God means trusting His providence.* The safety inherent in reverence springs from a state of dependence. The Grand Canyon is representative of the environment, just as the president is representative of the state. We depend on both for everything we have.

We depend far more fundamentally on God, in Whom "all things consist." In the Sermon of the Mount, Jesus is in no doubt as to Whom we should be thanking for our daily bread:

> Therefore take no thought, saying, What shall we eat? or, What shall we drink? or, Wherewithal shall we be clothed? (For after all these things do the Gentiles seek:) for your heavenly Father knoweth that ye have need of all these things. But seek ye first the kingdom of God, and his righteousness; and all these things shall be added unto you (Matthew 6:31-33).

The parallel passage in Luke goes on: "Fear not, little flock, for it is your Father's good pleasure to give you the kingdom" (Luke 12:32), and then proceeds to suggest a few practical ways of demonstrating fearlessness: "Sell that ye have, and give alms. . . ."

That "fear not" tolls like a signal bell through the pages of Scripture. The message is hammered home on over 300 separate occasions, in the Old Testament and the New. To fear God is to trust in His provision for your need. If you are a believer, God will meet your needs just as He met the needs of the Israelites when they journeyed in the wilderness. His promise is like a blank check given into your hands—a check which the fear of God will help you cash.

Time to decide

The whole problem of winning over fear boils down to one issue: whether or not you are willing to fear God. In the fear of God is contained, in embryo, the solution to all others. To fear God is to "fear not."

I emphasize the phrase "in embryo" because the spreading of this new kind of fear to the extremities of your being will take time, and will not become reality at all without your willing cooperation. You must give yourself to the task with the same commitment you would use in raising a child, or studying for a college degree. Without that patience and perseverance and determination you will probably give up. But I promise you this—in learning to fear God, you will receive not just victory over your fears, but many other blessings besides.

At this point, I want you to ask yourself two questions:

The first is: *Am I really honest enough to admit I have a fear?*

If you have read this far, I hope you are. I hope you have thought very carefully about fear and its disguises, and done your best to unmask it. But check all the same to make sure that it's not hiding away behind a screen of semantics. It is the easiest thing in the world to call your fear "prudence," or "caution," or some other fancy name. Lay it bare. Expose the fear for what it is.

The second question is: *Do I really want to win over my fear?*

Think carefully about that. Fear has some payoffs. It can give you a sense of worth, a false comaraderie at a coffee klatch, or material for conversation at a dinner meeting, in a Sunday School class, or over the backyard fence. You can talk about "great challenges" or "profound obstacles" or "serious threats." You can get a kick out of swapping fear stories with friends. If the stories are wild enough—about kids getting on drugs or having abortions, or about local racketeers threatening the community—you may obtain a certain notoriety in your little circle of friends.

There is a sense in which holding on to fear can give its own crazy, distorted, convoluted security. It is that security you will have to give up if you want to be rid of your fears. Winning over fear will mean leaving it behind forever. Are you sure you want to do that?

If you are, go on to the next page so we can get down to business.

9

The Timothy Formula

The key to winning over fear is to be found in the most fearful man in the New Testament.

His name is Timothy. He accompanied Paul on some of his journeys, and the apostle, who was not his real father, nonetheless seems to have developed a fatherly affection for him. Timothy took part in some important and dangerous missions across what is now Turkey and Greece. But he was a man with a problem, and his problem was fear.

Timothy's life exemplifies one of the most debilitating effects of fear—ineffectiveness. He seems to have been very gifted. God had set him apart for crucial work in the church, and for this work Paul and the elders had laid hands on him. Yet he fought constantly against the desire to hold back, to shy away. The word used of him, in fact, bears that particular meaning—timidity.

He was so sensitive that when Paul sent him to the troublesome church of Corinth, Paul also relayed special instructions to the church so that Timothy wouldn't be unduly disturbed by his reception:

> Now if Timotheus come, see that he may be with you without fear; for he worketh the work of the Lord, as I also do. Let no man therefore despise him: but conduct him forth in peace, that he may come unto me: for I look for him with the brethren (1 Corinthians 16:10,11).

There's no doubt Paul believed in Timothy's potential. The two letters he wrote to Timothy, which are preserved in the New Testament, are letters of encouragement and advice. But Paul knew of Timothy's weakness. The second epistle, written, it seems, to allay the young man's anxiety over Paul's imprisonment, overflows with assurance and concern:

> . . . I have remembrance of thee in my prayers
> night and day; greatly desiring to see thee, being
> mindful of thy tears, that I may be filled with joy;
> when I call to remembrance the unfeigned faith
> that is in thee, which dwelt first in thy grandmother
> Lois, and thy mother Eunice; and I am persuaded
> that in thee also. Wherefore I put thee in remem-
> brance that thou stir up the gift of God, which is in
> thee by the putting on of my hands (2 Timothy
> 1:3-6).

Apparently Timothy's fear had risen to such a pitch that he doubted his calling. He even doubted his faith. Fear was undermining his ministry, paralyzing him, preventing him from living and working effectively.

What is Paul's answer?

Well, he brings Timothy back to the fact of his faith—his fear of God. Through faith, he says, Timothy has been given all that he needs for a successful and victorious life. What about this timidity, this fear Timothy feels—is that a gift of God? Emphatically not, for "God hath not given us the spirit of fear; but of power, and of love, and of a sound mind" (2 Timothy 1:7).

Power, love, a sound mind (literally, self-control). That is the summary of Paul's solution to fear. Three gifts that are yours for free in the grace of God, if only you will take them. In the next three chapters I am going to look at them in more detail. Right now, I just want you to remember them. For convenience, I've expressed them in what I call the "Timothy Formula":

DYNAMISM + DEVOTION + DISCIPLINE =
DELIVERANCE FROM FEAR

Learn it and remember it, because it is the key to your victory over fear!

10

Deliverance Through Dynamism

Everyone wants power over fear. The sort of power dynamite has to blast rock out of a mine. The sort of power the dynamo has to generate electricity. The power of dynamism.

Is this power to be found inside you? There are many people around who will try to persuade you it is. A central technique employed by psychologists in the treatment of fear is called "behavior modification." The theory is quite simple—you put the fearing person into the very situation that makes him afraid, and then teach him to respond to it differently. Up to a point it works. A man told to tackle his fear of big bridges by traveling repeatedly over small ones can now manage a four-mile span. Some people terrified by airplanes can now journey by air.

But it only works up to a point. A report in *Business Week* (April 21, 1986) says of this form of therapy, used to treat phobias at a clinic in Rockville, that "for many phobics 'cure' is a relative term. Psychologist Ross reminds patients that phobias can reappear months or even years after seemingly successful therapy. The aim of therapy, she says, is to give sufferers 'the ability to lead a normal life without avoidance.'"

In other words, the power offered is of a very limited sort. The strategy aims not so much to eradicate fear as to contain it. And for this open-ended solution to your problem you can, according to *Business Week*, pay up to $1,300 for a 16-week course.

Now in case you haven't clued in already, I'll say again that winning over fear God's way will involve you in much more than four months of therapy sessions. What God asks of you is a complete turnaround in your values, priorities, and lifestyle. Some people will make the mistake of seeing this as a "price" for treatment, as though God expected them to repay

Him by going to church on Sunday or turning religious. It is not. What God gives, He gives entirely free. The transformation of your whole person is not the cost of the treatment, but the means by which it is effected. You win over fear by becoming a new person under God. If you refuse that transformation, you may still find some help with your fear, but you will never really win over it.

The reason is clear when you think about the resources at your disposal. On your own you have simply yourself, your own determination and strength of character. That isn't enough. If it were, you wouldn't have a problem with fear, and you wouldn't be reading this now. All right, then—let's assume you pay your $1,300 and go to consult a leading authority on fears and phobias. He recommends therapy. What have you got now? The same as you always had, with a teaspoon of psychological method and maybe a pinch of extra confidence. In short, nothing has really changed.

By way of contrast, I'll give you a snatch preview of the "dynamism" in the Timothy Formula.

Paul talks about it in the first chapter of Ephesians. His prayer for the Ephesian church is what I pray for you:

> That the God of our Lord Jesus Christ, the Father of glory, may give unto you the spirit of wisdom and revelation in the knowledge of him: The eyes of your understanding being enlightened; that ye may know what is the hope of his calling, and what is the riches of the glory of his inheritance in the saints, and what is the exceeding greatness of his power to us-ward who believe, according to the working of his mighty power, Which he wrought in Christ, when he raised him from the dead, and set him at his own right hand in the heavenly places, far above all principality, and power, and might, and dominion, and every name that is named, not only in this world, but also in that which is to come: And hath put all things under his feet (Ephesians 1:17-22).

You can tell how enthusiastic Paul is about God's dynamism—he doesn't stop long enough to end a sentence!

Read it over again, slowly. Let it soak into you. This power Paul is writing about is the power God is ready to release into your war against fear. Paul could hardly have found a stronger term to describe it than "exceeding greatness." It is the same power that brought the world into being, and governs the motion of the universe. It is the same power that sliced open the Red Sea, and moved in a pillar of cloud before the tribes of Israel. It is the same power that raised Jesus Christ from the dead, and set Him in the place of highest authority, putting everything under His dominion. We are not in the playpen here. Thermonuclear warheads, the sun, or the accumulated energy of the entire cosmos cannot begin to compare with the power of God.

No wonder Paul later describes God as "him that is able to do exceeding abundantly above all that we ask or think, according to the power that worketh in us . . ." (Ephesians 3:20). Such power, active in the lives of ordinary men and women like us, cannot fail to exceed our expectations. And since fear comes under the heading of "all things," there is no doubt that victory is ours through faith in God.

Power at work

I said earlier that Paul was subject to a great many rational fears. I am convinced that no one could have endured the stress he did who was not filled with this dynamism, this power of God. But how did the power work in practice?

Paul gives us a tantalizing insight in his letters to the Corinthian Church. Take this excerpt from his description of the work of an apostle:

> We are hard pressed on every side, yet not crushed; we are perplexed, but not in despair; persecuted, but not forsaken; struck down, but not destroyed—always carrying about in the body the dying of the Lord Jesus, that the life of Jesus also

may be manifested in our body.

For we who live are always delivered to death for Jesus' sake, that the life of Jesus also may be manifested in our mortal flesh. So then death is working in us, but life in you.

But since we have the same spirit of faith, according to what is written, "I believed and therefore I spoke," we also believe and therefore speak, knowing that He who raised up the Lord Jesus will also raise us up with Jesus, and will present us with you.

For all things are for your sakes, that grace, having spread through the many, may cause thanksgiving to abound to the glory of God.

Therefore we do not lose heart. But though our outward man is perishing, yet the inward man is being renewed day by day.

For our light affliction, which is but for a moment, is working for us a far more exceeding and eternal weight of glory, while we do not look at the things which are seen, but at the things which are not seen. For the things which are seen are temporary, but the things which are not seen are eternal (2 Corinthians 4:8-18 NKJV).

Notice how Paul's entire outlook is transformed. He doesn't overcome his fear by using a psychological technique—the overcoming is implicit in the transformation. Consequently, though he feels fear as a natural God-given faculty for recognizing danger, he doesn't suffer illegitimate fear. That death is "at work" in him, through constant risk and stress, is relatively unimportant. Provided he is serving the church, and God is being glorified, his present hardships are a mere "light affliction." Like clouds, they are here today and will be gone tomorrow.

Not many of us would describe what he went through as a "light affliction." But for Paul such dangers were a seeding bed where the power of God could grow. "I can do all things through Christ which strengthens me," he wrote to the Philippians, ". . . and my God shall supply all your need according to his riches in glory by Christ Jesus" (Philippians 4:13,19). Was he comfortably ensconced in a posh penthouse apartment when he said that, or sitting in some magnificent Roman high-rise in a recliner, watching color TV? Was he munching on chocolates, writing his letter with a $150 gold pen, under a six-way lamp, on nonglare paper? Hardly! When Paul said, "I can do all things," he was cooped up in one of Nero's cells awaiting execution.

The Western mind rebels at that concept. To us it seems only good sense for a man in Paul's position to go about his business using the most comfortable divine gifts of wealth and influence. We cannot understand how "I can do all things" goes hand in hand with total powerlessness. We cannot understand how the attainment of goals is furthered by perpetual exposure to danger and pain. Yet for Paul the two are as inseparable as magnets. He was happy to forgo even the blessing of health for the sake of the kingdom. Why? Because the greater his weakness, the greater his capacity to receive the power of God:

> Therefore I take pleasure in infirmities, in reproaches, in necessities, in persecutions, in distresses for Christ's sake: for when I am weak, then am I strong (2 Corinthians 12:10).

This topsy-turvy logic has some pretty shattering implications, though I am not concerned with those now. I emphasize the point only to make it clear that God's dynamism is not available to us because we are strong, but rather because we are weak. And the weaker we are, the more available it is.

It follows that we must be honest about our weakness. It is a universal human failing to put on a brave face and pretend everything is okay when it plainly isn't. Assuming that sort of "power" for the sake of keeping up appearances only compounds the problem by preventing us from receiving the real power. We are doing ourselves no service if we talk down our fear instead of facing up to it as a weakness. Paul was so determined not to lead the Corinthians into this particular error that he deliberately exposed himself to fears in order to show that it was God, and not he, who had the power over them:

> I was with you in weakness, and in fear, and in much trembling . . . that your faith should not stand in the wisdom of men, but in the power of God (1 Corinthians 2:3,5).

Paul knew Who was the Source of that power and how important it was to stay "plugged in" by faith in Christ. Take the plug out, and the lamp will fail. Keep it in, and a light is shed that drives back every shadow of fear. Think of every bad experience that could ever happen to you—contemplate all of your worst fears—and you will still be able to say with Paul, ". . . in all these things we are more than conquerors through him that loved us" (Romans 8:30).

When I was a boy, I read the story of the martyrdom of John and Betty Stamm. It made an indelible impression on me. They were beheaded, but by all accounts they remained calm and serene right up to the moment of their execution. That was the spirit of dynamism.

The Christian superperson

Finally, let me add a word of caution.

I have used Paul as an example of dynamism because his circumstances and his faith are painted in the Scripture with bold colors. The two together make a striking combination. But I am aware that by doing this I run the risk of reinforcing a minor heresy of the evangelical churches, namely that Paul is a champion of faith who should be imitated in every possible respect.

Clearly there are many ways in which we should imitate him. He invited believers to do that. But God's dynamism in Paul, like God's dynamism in everyone else, is to some extent a unique phenomenon. We are not all meant to be miniature Pauls or Paulines. The Bible doesn't commend uniformity of character and gifts, and in practical terms, for everyone to strive for the sort of personal dynamism that Paul had is as ridiculous as using all the power in your house for toasters and nothing else. So I'd like to explode the myth of the forthright, extroverted, omnicompetent Christian superperson. You can be dynamic and ungodly, just as you can be reserved and deeply spiritual! I doubt whether Paul himself would have matched our mental stereotype if we'd met him. So why lay so much stress on appearances?

God's dynamism does not necessarily result in a "dynamic" personality. It may do so, but it is important to recognize that the quiet person can be filled with God's power just as easily as the loud and boisterous one, only in a more low-key and unpretentious way. To go back to the analogy of electricity, some people are toasters, others are lights, still others are burglar alarms. Someone may be an electric toothbrush. It doesn't really matter—the important point is that you are to be filled with God's power to perform your own special task.

Of course, right now your purpose in plugging into God's power is to tackle your fear. We have seen that weakness is no obstacle to that. In fact, if we take Paul's example seriously, it appears that weakness provides the opportunity to use God's power.

But if Paul had written to Timothy, "Fear is overcome by power," none of us would be much further along. We need something to get a grip on dynamism, a handle on the drill to help us use it.

That handle is love.

11

Deliverance Through Devotion

I am calling love "devotion" for a special purpose.

Love, in common parlance, is fast losing the rich flavor of meaning it possesses in the Bible. A character on a TV drama is likely to tell a women he loves her, and ten minutes later be suing for divorce. I don't deny that the scriptwriter had in mind a strong emotion when he used the word "love." The problem is he never went beyond it. The same happened in the '60's and early '70's when love was taken up as a political slogan. Everyone agreed with the Beatles that "all we need is love," but because love was understood as an emotion, it had about as much effect on world affairs as throwing feathers at a tank.

Love is more than emotion. It involves commitment. You know that well enough if you have children. People without children are apt to sentimentalize family life, as though it were all beach parties and barbecues. Now I'm a great believer in the family, but I also know that parents are put to the test. There are times when children are desperately annoying, when they get under your feet, break windows in the greenhouse, or ask you to do something at the moment you're stepping out the door. If love were all emotion it would be conspicuously absent at a time like that! But, in fact, it isn't absent. We love our children even when they drive us crazy. We are committed to them.

It is this committed love I am calling devotion. But how does this committed love, this devotion, help us as a "handle" for power? Well, the answer starts not with our devotion, but with God's.

Know you are loved

The same distinction I have made between emotional love and committed love also applies to God.

I don't know how many times I've heard people say "God is love," or something similar, as though the existence of a benign Old Man snoring gently on a cloud of cotton wool was supposed to be a comfort to the sick and suffering. Is God's love so remote He pays no attention to evil, injustice, and cruelty? Or is He blithely sleeping through it all? Let's assume for a moment that this God is not asleep, but that He cares enough about His human family to intervene when evil gets the upper hand. What might He do, if His love were ruled directly by His emotions?

The answer is difficult to think about. After all, God's family hasn't paid much attention to Him over the years. If we are annoyed by the occasional disobedience of our children, just imagine the weight of provocation that bears on our heavenly Father. Why on earth should he still love us? Look what happened in the days of Noah: "God saw that the wickedness of man was great in the earth. . . . And the Lord said, I will destroy man whom I have created" (Genesis 6:5,7).

God, after that single act of judgment, tempered justice with forbearance because of the commitment of His love. In Hebrew, there is a special word for it, translated in the King James Version as "kindness," "loving kindness," and "mercy." It means love with commitment, love that does not walk out when the other party gives offense. It is used frequently, for there are plenty of times in the Old Testament when God's people push His patience to the limit:

> Nevertheless my loving kindness will I not utterly take from him, nor suffer my faithfulness to fail. My covenant will I not break, nor alter the thing that is gone out of my lips (Psalm 89:33,34).

God's devotion, in fact, is what turned the Old Testament into the New, what makes Christian faith possible. As Paul says in Romans, "God commendeth his love towards us, in that, while we were yet sinners, Christ died for us" (Romans 5:8). Mere emotional love is incapable of commitment like that. It turns aside and says of the disobedient, "They've made their bed—now they can lie in it!" If God's love had been a matter of feelings, there would have been no incarnation, no cross, no redemption.

But Christ died. God acted in expression of His love for us though we had done nothing to deserve it. And this action had two effects.

First, it provided concrete evidence that God cares for us. I'm not talking about the sleepy benignity of the Old Man on his cotton wool cloud. "Care" here is the kind of practical love and support a father extends to his children, watching out for them, protecting them, ensuring the best for them, even— and I don't say it lightly—disciplining them if they go astray. Trust in the Father's devotion to us is what Jesus encouraged when He said, "Come unto me, all ye that labor and are heavy laden, and I will give you rest" (Matthew 11:28). Peter advocates it in his first epistle: "Humble yourselves, therefore, under the mighty hand of God . . . Casting all your care upon him; for he careth for you" (1 Peter 5:6,7). And, of course, Paul refers to it in that famous passage from Romans 8:

> We know that all things work together for good to them that love God, to them who are the called according to his purpose. For whom he did foreknow, he also did predestinate to be conformed to the image of his Son, that he might be the firstborn among many brethren (Romans 8:28,29).

So be assured that whatever fears you face, you face them in company with your heavenly Father. In the crucifixion, Jesus faced reduction of human fear. He knows what it's like, and He overcame it. Nothing that will happen to you in the future, none of those fear-scenarios you toy with in your mind, will come to pass unless the experience is for your ultimate good. Take comfort from that.

Make love your aim

The second effect of God's love expressed in Jesus is to provide us with an example to follow. And it is in the following of this example that we have our handle on the power of God.

Example is really too mild a word. To love was the only one of Jesus' instructions He called a commandment. Listen to Him talking to His disciples on the night of the Last Supper:

> "This is my commandment, that ye love one another, as I have loved you. Greater love hath no man than this, that a man lay down his life for his friends . . . . These things I command you, that ye love one another (John 15:12,13,17).

Once again, this love is more than emotion. Jesus isn't asking us to generate mushy feelings for each other. It isn't even good enough to talk about love, as though saying it were the same as doing it. "Greater love hath no man than this, that a man *lay down his life for his friends*." The love God wants us to have is a practical love, the self-giving love Jesus showed us on the cross. Without that practical expression, the love in us will be as meaningless as the electrical signals in a telephone wire are without an earpiece to turn them into words. Unexpressed, love is unintelligible.

This love, which I am calling devotion, is distinguished by its own Greek word in the New Testament—*agape*. My own personal definition of *agape* is "the outgoing of the totality of your being to another in beneficence and help." Almost invariably the writers of the epistles unpack it like a suitcase, to show you what is really inside.

> Put on therefore, as the elect of God, holy and beloved, bowels of mercies, kindness, humbleness of mind, meekness, longsuffering; forbearing one another, and forgiving one another, if any man have a quarrel against any: even as Christ forgave you, so also do ye.
>
> And above all these things put on charity, which is the bond of perfectness (Colossians 3:12-14).

So love is something we do, not something we feel. But how does that help us use the power of God to overcome fear?

It helps in three ways.

1. *Love repels fear.* In his first epistle John says, "There is no fear in love, but perfect love casteth out fear" (1 John 4:18). In other words, there is a quality about love itself that dissolves fear as the sun melts the winter snow. As Albert Barnes says in his commentary:

> Nothing will do more to inspire courage, to make a man fearless of danger, or ready to endure privation and persecution, than love. The love of country, and wife, and children, and home, makes the most timid bold when they are assailed, and the love of Christ and of a dying world nerves the soul to great enterprises, and sustains it in the deepest sorrows (*Notes on the New Testament*, 1949).

2. *Love directs the attention outward.* Fear is fundamentally selfish and introspective. When I am afraid, I fear something that is going to happen to me. Even when I am afraid for someone I love, my fear contemplates my own suffering, my own bereavement. Fear turns me in on myself.

By contrast, devotion is outer-directed. In loving, you find your attention taken up with the happiness and welfare of others. This has the salutary effect of putting your own worries in perspective, for it is the easiest thing in the world, when you are looking inward, to think your fears are unique. Being outer-directed also means, very often, that your mind is buzzing so loud with other people's interests that you simply don't have time to be afraid.

And what if you have a *Big Bad Wolf fear*, where the other person is actually the object of the fear? Well, love helps there, too, because when you love someone you begin to see the difference between the person and the twisted circumstances that have placed him in a position of animosity towards you. "Father, forgive them," said Jesus as the soldiers nailed him to the cross, "for they know not what they do" (Luke 23:34).

The evangelist David Wilkerson found that love helped him in this way when he came face-to-face with the gang leader Nicki Cruz. That gang leader became a friend and colleague. So remember, you may find that loving an enemy makes him into a friend. You might just find he wasn't an enemy in the first place!

3. *Love brings its own reward*. In modern psychiatric jargon I'd reexpress this as "love produces positive feedback." Isn't that a bit selfish? Not really. *Big Bad Wolf fear*, particularly, is encouraged by lack of communication. Haven't you ever heard somebody say, "I don't like so-and-so, she doesn't smile much." I wonder what so-and-so would think if she knew what an effect her gloomy face was having on her colleagues! Devotion expressed in something as simple as a smile can open up bridges of communication and end the negative interaction that fosters suspicion and fear on both sides.

The trigger

Devotion that releases dynamism is part of the transformation the Holy Spirit works in the life of the believer. It undermines the foundations on which fear is built and sets up a new structure in the personality of assurance and trust, against which fear is powerless.

But this structure does not build itself. The Spirit may be the architect, but you are the foreman, and this means that you must have a conscious determination to keep at the job. Maybe you find that a bit daunting. "The problem," you say, "is that it's so hard. Like Nehemiah rebuilding the walls of Jerusalem under the eye of his enemies, I find I'm constantly distracted by my fears."

Well, I am going to show you how you can turn that very fact to your advantage.

Many kinds of fear—and especially *Big Bad Wolf fear*, where the fear-object is rejection by others—come to us, as it were, "on cue." Fear, after all, is a warning signal. It is meant to alert us to danger. So imagine your fear is associated with your boss at the office. Your fear-object is rejection (a snub, a lost promotion), and your fear-scenario is any sort of confrontation with your supervisor. Looked at rationally, the boss is about as much fun as a sore toe. But he is not an ogre. You would be able to handle him if only you hadn't developed an *exaggerated fear* of meeting him.

In that kind of situation you can use devotion directly—not just as a new lifestyle that makes you strong against fear, but as a way of addressing yourself to particular fear-objects. All you need do is determine that whenever you feel the fear, you will put love into action. When the boss comes into the room, instead of ignoring him, say, "Hi! How are you?" Do that, and you will have won a decisive victory over your fear. Why? Because you've given it a new role. You've turned fear into a reminder to love.

I used the image of the handle on the power drill to describe the relationship of dynamism and devotion. When you use fear as a reminder to love, it becomes the trigger. You win over fear by making it work for you. Before, when fear came, you used to say to yourself, "Oh dear, I'd forgotten about that until you reminded me." Now you can say, "Thanks! If you hadn't shown up I'd have missed a chance to show love!"

Redeployed in this way, fear turns up some unexpected benefits. The criticism of others suddenly appears as a free education in improving our performance. The betrayal of friends becomes a chance to show thought for others. And, not surprisingly, many anticipated rejections are averted because our own behavior is no longer reinforcing the pattern of rejection.

Let me illustrate.

When I was 12 years old, my father took me to Camp Barakel, where he was chaplain and main counselor. One day we had to drive to Battle Creek, Michigan, about 50 miles away, but hadn't gone 14 miles before the car stopped. We had run out of gas. This was extraordinary because we'd just filled up. Dad got out to take a look. He soon found the problem. Somebody had driven a spike into the gas tank.

This was a blow. In 1936 Dad's weekly income, which had to feed a family of five, was slightly more than half of what today's American government reckons as the minimum wage. He and my mother certainly lived on faith! The car was an old jalopy, a 1930 Chevrolet. I sometimes say to people that we worked on that car from Monday through Saturday so we could drive it on Sunday. Yet we couldn't have done without it.

As soon as I saw the damage I knew who was responsible. He was a miserable little rascal, a double-distilled bully, and a cocky, incorrigible troublemaker. I wasn't alone in my loathing for him. But when I exploded to Dad, he scolded me and told me not to jump to conclusions.

Fortunately, Dad was able to get help on the highway. We returned to the camp for dinner, but I didn't eat. As the oldest child in the family, I was always concerned about the family finances, and I couldn't imagine how Dad was going to get money to replace the gas tank and fill up for the journey home. My fear turned into hostility when I saw Dad perched on the edge of the dock with his arm around the shoulders of the same little monster who had spiked his tank.

I could not understand Dad's attitude. Yet it is my view now, more than half a century later, that Dad's response made a positive and lasting impression on the boy. He was revealing the spirit of the Lord Jesus. He had every reason not to— he was a young man with three growing boys and a wife whose sickness put a constant drain on funds. He could have let fear of impoverishment drive him into a rage. But he subdued his fear, and turned it into an opportunity for love.

In 1972, I was conducting meetings in the public buildings in Portugal. During that time, the chairman of the crusade, Mr. Matthys Van den Heuvel, hosted a black-tie banquet for the leaders of business, government, education, religion, the media, the professions and the arts. It was as elegant and impeccably executed an affair as I've ever attended. The purpose of Mr. Van den Heuvel and his wife was to present the gospel of Christ Jesus.

I was delighted and surprised at the eager interest of the audience in the teachings of the Bible. After the program was over, the Swiss representative (in Portugal) of one of the large Swiss pharmeceutical companies walked up to Mrs. Van den Heuvel, a raven-haired Swiss lady of high standing who, along with her husband, subjugated everything they were and had to the communication of the gospel.

"This has been a fascinating experience for me," he said. "You have given me the opportunity to meet people I have long wanted to meet. I must tell you, though, I am an atheist."

Mrs. Van den Heuvel looked him in the eye, smiled graciously and said, "Oh, I am sorry."

"Why are you sorry?"

"Because God is so big, and you are so little, and you will need Him. And you don't even know where to go for help. I feel so sorry for you. I will pray for you."

His eyes widened. I learned a lesson from that. Mrs. Van den Heuvel didn't try to rebut him. She didn't argue. She didn't give him a polemic on the resurrection of Christ. She just showed genuine Christian compassion and love in a way that man could not ignore.

She might easily have succumbed to fear. She might have thought, "Here's this man, one of the most important foreign businessmen in Portugal. He is well connected. Since we are both Swiss, he may belittle me when he sees our mutual friends in Switzerland. He may think I'm a fanatic."

None of that. She simply turned the temptation to fear into an opportunity for love—and who knows what effect that had on the man's eternal destiny?

Using fear as a trigger works even on very extreme fears.

A while ago, a woman was attacked and raped in Atlanta by a group of young felons. It was the kind of attack that could leave enduring scars and cause petrifying fear every time an unknown man said good morning to her, be it in a country club or a church, an office or a school. Those scars never appeared, because she turned the temptation to fear into an opportunity to love. She forgave the men and made known to them her concern for their conversion. It had a powerful impact on them, and it released her from the traumas of fear.

I had a friend in Grand Rapids, Michigan, whose wife, eight-year-old son and and baby daughter were murdered by the man who was rooming with them. The 1929 depression wasn't long past. The boarder was an educator; he had needed accommodation, and my friend had needed the money.

It would have seemed natural, after the triple murder, for my friend to fear for the safety of loved ones every time he left home. But no. Instead, he started writing to the murderer and even paid him an occasional visit at the Michigan State penitentiary. He did it for 50 years. And far from being scarred by fear, my friend was one of the most radiant men I have ever known. He had won over fear through love.

I am absolutely convinced that the answer to fear in all shattered relationships is love. Joseph, who rose from slavery in Egypt to second in command to Pharaoh, was reconciled to the brothers who had abducted him as a child. He might still have feared them years later when they appeared before him as victims of famine, asking for grain. He might have been prompted by fear to turn them away empty-handed. But he was not. He used the temptation to fear as an opportunity to love.

In all broken relationships, fear can be won over by love. Children who suffered abuse from their parents can win over fear. So can the victims of abuse in marriage—and I mean men as well as women. John Wesley suffered abuse from his wife. She threw hot coffee in his face, pulled him up by his hair, and humiliated him before those he was preaching to. Yet the very fact that history has forgotten Mrs. Wesley is testimony to the power Wesley had over his fear. Like Joseph, he turned the temptation to fear into an opportunity to love.

But, of course, that doesn't come about by magic. Fear may be the trigger on the power drill of dynamism, but it's up to you to press it. If fear comes along, and you don't turn it into opportunity, you are back where you started. So how do you take yourself in hand?

12

Deliverance Through Discipline

Dynamism, devotion and discipline aren't three separate techniques from which you make a selection or rejection according to a whim of the moment. They form a single coordinated approach to the problem of fear. Apart from the other components, each one is about as much use as a single player on a football field.

You could summarize their relationship like this: "To apply dynamism through devotion requires discipline."

Discipline is the quarterback of the outfit. Without it, nothing works. Of course, inspired by pity or conscience, you can practice devotion on the spur of the moment. If a member of your church congregation is dying in the hospital, for instance, you might make a mental resolution to visit him once a week. Assuming he lasts only a month, you will have no trouble keeping the promise. But what if he has a remission? Will that original impulse of love or pity keep you driving to the hospital every Sunday afternoon for two years? I doubt it! In order to maintain your commitment you will need a motivating force that does not fade—a quarterback who keeps the team organized right to the end of the game.

But there lies the problem with discipline. "If I cannot rely on love to motivate me," you say, "how can I be sure of exercising the required discipline? Might I not wake up one morning and think, 'Today I really can't be bothered with this?' Where is my discipline then?"

My answer is that you are thinking of discipline in the wrong way. Naturally, you cannot be certain how you will feel on any given day in the future. More likely than not, on some days you will prefer to neglect your commitments and do something to please yourself. But discipline isn't a *feeling* that you ought to do your duty. Such feelings, if you get them,

117

originate in your conscience. They will prompt you, but they can never force you to do something you are "not in the mood for" or "can't be bothered with."

Discipline is a momentum of good habits. It is easier to push a moving car than to move a stalled one. Discipline is like that. It is harder to overcome the initial inertia, but it gets easier as the new habits sink deeper and deeper into your personality. Eventually the momentum is so great that stopping is harder than continuing. Consequently when I talk about developing discipline, I am not trying to infuse you with a new state of mind, a new feeling, or a new way of looking at commitments. I am recommending a set of positive actions which, with about the same amount of effort you would put into jump-starting a car with the cable connections to a power source, you can use to get your spiritual life moving under its own power.

I know that God is the source of all true power. That doesn't release you from personal effort and responsibility. God gives you breath, but *you* must do the breathing. He doesn't do it for you.

These positive actions all work toward the same objective—opening your life and consciousness to the Holy Spirit. There are two reasons for this.

One, the love through which dynamism is released cannot be generated by your own willpower. Let's face it. Most of us do a poor job of loving even our friends and family, let alone those who make us afraid. Are you really capable of loving an intimidating boss, your critical colleagues, or the men who wrecked your home in a burglary with an open, self-giving love? Not in your own human strength. We need the vital, renewing touch of the Holy Spirit on our lives if God's amazing transformation is going to set us free from our fears.

Two, discipline in spiritual matters is the foundation for all other disciplines. You cannot hope to have the self-control necessary to win over fear if you are not willing to learn the discipline of fellowship with God, whose love is the antidote to all fear. Be disciplined in your relationship with God, and self-control in other areas will follow naturally.

Five divisions of discipline

1. *Quiet time*. The most powerful countermeasure against fear is the awareness of walking in fellowship with God. That's why beginning each day with a quiet time is so essential.

Let me put before you this question. If Jesus were with you in His human form and promised to live in your home, go with you wherever you went, advise you on every decision, and personally encourage you during every depression— would you then suffer fear? I don't think you would. Now consider what Paul meant when he wrote to the Colossians about "Christ in you, the hope of glory" (Colossians 1:27). He is not with us; He is *in* us. God has sent His Holy Spirit to guide us into all truth, to undergird us with power, to illuminate us with His light.

"But that's not the same as seeing Him," you say.

I agree—it's better! All you need do is draw the benefits of God's presence within you. The best way to start is by the disciplined use of your quiet time.

I once traveled for three weeks with Dr. and Mrs. Han Kyung Chik of Korea. Every morning they were up at five o'clock for the dawn prayer meeting. This man—pastor, educator, humanitarian, statesman, author—not only begins his day with at least one hour of quiet time, but he bows his head inconspicuously in prayer before every activity, event, and conversation. I have watched him visit businessmen in their offices. He would sit down, and for perhaps 15 seconds he would quietly bow his head and close his eyes. I knew he was committing that particular conversation to the Lord.

What a deterrent to fear! What a guarantee for God's victory! I have no doubt that Dr. Han's serenity, after a life of harassment by the Communists (who on several occasions dispossessed him and chased him out of home and town) can be attributed to his quiet time with God. His face is a mosaic of cheerful calm.

What does a quiet time consist of? Chiefly, two elements: prayer and Bible study. It is a time of communing with God, being in His presence in an undisturbed and conscious way. If you are married, or have a good friend, you will know what it is like simply to be with somebody you are close to. Contact doesn't depend on words alone. Yet words are important. There are matters we want to make known to God, wrongs we want to confess, blessings for which we want to give thanks. And there are promptings from the Holy Spirit that we hear either in meditation or through reading God's Word, the Bible.

Bible study, of course, doesn't have to be tied into a personal quiet time any more than prayer does. I applaud a group of high-powered young businessmen in Atlanta who meet for a Bible study every Friday morning. They find it inspiring and mind-broadening to cross denominational barriers to fellowship with their peers in the study of God's Word. I have talked to some of these men, and have every reason to conclude that God uses this Friday morning Bible study to still their hearts and to dissipate the fears arising from their professional concerns.

I could go into a lot more detail on both aspects of the quiet time. I won't, because I've covered the topic extensively elsewhere. If you want further guidance I suggest you look up the fourth section in *How to Win Over Worry*, where I devote four chapters specifically to prayer. Remember, quiet time is a key to victory over fear.

2. *Fellowship.* One of the blessings of the Friday morning study group I referred to is that it combines fellowship with God and fellowship with others.

That second sort of fellowship is important. Contemporary society—especially in America, with her frenetic lifestyle and TV churches—too easily squeezes out fellowship with others. But the Bible clearly teaches that no Christian is an island. It isn't an unwarranted distortion of the text to render 1 John 4:20 as follows: "How can you say you love God whom you have not seen, when you have no fellowship with your brothers whom you have seen?"

At the time of this writing my father is 90 years old. He attends Sunday school faithfully. He hasn't missed a week since 1923. Even when he was in the hospital for surgery, one of the classes he taught met in his hospital room so he would be able to keep up his record and minister to the business and professional men who make up his class. Dad attends every Sunday morning worship service, every Sunday evening service, every Wednesday night prayer meeting. He attends every church function including revival meetings and Bible study weeks.

In his knowledge of the Bible, and of Greek and Hebrew, Dad is probably the equal, if not superior, to any of the ministers to whom he listens or for whom he prays. His pastor, Dr. J. Hoffman Harris, who built the church from a handful of people to a membership of over five thousand while founding 27 thriving daughter churches, would be the first to agree to that. And yet Dad is unstinting in his praise for the younger man. "I don't believe there is anywhere in the world a man more compassionate and more gifted in the area of pastoral leadership than Dr. Harris," he exults.

Dad lives alone. He drives his own car and takes care of his own meals. He speaks an average of three times a week. He prays for long periods at the break of each day. He has read the Bible through 102 times. But he does not allow that to anesthetize him with the needle of smugness, or seduce him with the idea that his background or advancing years exempt him from the need for fellowship.

Though he is 25 years past normal retiring age he displays no evidence of fear. I attribute this remarkable lifestyle to discipline that touches every area of his life—quiet time, physical exercise, dietary control, reading, memorizing, and so on. But it is his fellowship with others that I believe keeps him youthful in spirit and attractive to other people. When a group of youngsters went on retreat recently, they insisted on taking him along. He was the center of attention. They marveled that he could play the piano, and marveled even more that he could play the cornet at the same time!

We all need fellowship, and we all benefit from it. On one occasion when my wife and I were relaxing for a couple of days in Florida, we attended the Wednesday night prayer service of the First Baptist Church. Dr. Avery, for years the senior pastor, squinted his eyes as he looked in my direction. Finally he said, "Is that John Haggai I see back there?"

I assured him it was.

He then went off into an effusive expression of appreciation that we had come to the meeting, and bemoaned the fact that so few people on vacation followed our example. I was downright embarrassed! We had come because we felt we needed to come, because we wanted fellowship. Dr. Avery was loading us up with laurels we didn't deserve.

The point is that fellowship enriches not only the lives of others, but your own life as well. And that is a powerful ally against fear.

3. *Testimony.* I can't explain it, nor can I back up my argument with chapter and verse, but I have been convinced for some time that those who exercise the discipline of telling what God has done for them receive, whether or not they realize it, a freedom from fear.

Testimony reinforces faith, and fear cannot cohabit with faith.

I think of the late R. G. Le Tourneau, inventor and manufacturer of earth-moving equipment. He would come to my crusades in the '50's and '60's and give his testimony on a Saturday night. No matter where this man was, he would talk about the Lord. I think of Bob Glaze, the Dallas businessman and civic leader; Paul Meyer, the president of the Success Motivation Institute; John Bolten, a multinational businessman living in Germany; and Otto Bohl, the European investment banker—men who discuss their faith as easily as they discuss their families. Observing these men convinces me they are free from fears that hold so many men hostage.

Businessmen Stanley Tam has testified by writing a book about his Christian odyssey. You read between the lines of his book robust faith, not wretched fear. I've never met Stanley Tam, but I was in Toronto recently to address a group of business and professional people, and at my table two men (one of Canada's leading developers, and the Canadian head of Apple Computer) mentioned his name. They told of the powerful impact Stanley Tam had made on them. They were fascinated by his life and witness, and wanted to know more about him.

When I talk about giving testimony, incidentally, I'm not referring to those earnest believers who testify only in religious circles, at church services and convocations. I mean those who do their testifying "in their stride," who are able to integrate testimony into their everyday conversation as naturally as they would the weather, the World Series, or Soviet-American relations. In many ways, testifying on home ground is too easy. When you talk about your faith to those outside the cozy confines of the church, you are taking a far greater personal risk. And even though I am sure that those who testify in this way do not publicize their spiritual experience in order to overcome fear, years of observation have shown me that it has this effect.

I heartily recommend, therefore, that you make it part of your spiritual discipline to witness naturally and easily about what the Lord has done in your life.

4. *Obedience.* Not everyone is brilliant. Not everyone has a high IQ. Not everyone is handsome or beautiful. Not everyone is well-connected socially or from a famous family. Not everyone is wealthy, charming, or sensitive. But anybody, anybody at all, can be obedient.

Obedience dissipates fear, just as disobedience fosters it. Think of Saul in the Old Testament. God had told him not to bring back any livestock from the enemy camp. He disobeyed. He could not resist taking a few of the prize cattle and the best sheep. When the prophet Samuel demanded an explanation, Saul began a long and sanctimonious diatribe on how God had blessed him and given him victory in battle. Samuel cut in with a truth that, to his dying day, Saul never really grasped: "To obey is better than sacrifice, and to hearken than the fat of rams" (1 Samuel 15:22).

Study the life of Saul and I think you will agree he was a man dominated by fear. There was no observable reason for him to be afraid. Physically, he stood head and shoulders above his companions. Vocationally, God had picked him out for leadership. Spiritually, in his life and leadership role, he enjoyed the mentoring of the prophet Samuel. Financially, he was rich. He had everything going for him. Why was it he fell into the clutches of fear? There is only one explanation—disobedience.

On the other hand look at the experience of Dr. Harry Ironside. Almost 60 years ago Moody Memorial Church asked Dr. Ironside to become its pastor. Since Dr. Ironside worshiped with the Plymouth Brethren, this put him on the spot. The Brethren do not believe in an ordained clergy. They believe in the priesthood of all believers, which to them means that any member of the church, and not just the pastor, can bring a message to the meeting.

Dr. Ironside had a real battle with his conscience. He told his friends, "I received this call from Moody, and in prayer I said, 'Lord, what about the Brethren?' Yet a second time the call came, and once again I asked the Lord, 'Lord, what about the Brethren?' A third time the call came from Moody for me to become the pastor, and I asked, 'Lord, what about the Brethren?' It was then that the Lord said to me, 'Harry, you go to Moody, and I'll take care of the Brethren.' "

The Brethren always respected Dr. Ironside, and he always loved them. But he had to obey, and in obedience he had victory over his fears. I had the pleasure of knowing Dr. Ironside. My wife was one of his favorite soloists. He requested her to do solo work at his anniversary services when she was in Chicago. I am still impressed, favorably impressed, with his easy demeanor and his continuing victory over fear—a victory which, being privy to some of his devastating personal heartaches, I know wasn't cheap.

God asks hard decisions of all of us from time to time. Believe me, the right way is always the way of obedience. It may not seem like it at the time, but the road God takes you on will always bring you safely through your fears.

5. *Service.* My mother never knew good health. She suffered from pernicious anemia, emphysema and angina, among many other ailments.

Forty-five years before her death the doctors said she would not live. She lived to be 80 years old. And throughout the course of her life, with great discipline, she served others. My father said that she could write legibly in such small handwriting that she cheated the post office back in the days of the one-cent postcard! She could get more on a postcard than most people can in a letter. Into her later years she kept up her correspondence with friends all over the world, a constant stream of messages that gave hope, encouragement, and spiritual counsel.

From the human standpoint mother had every reason to be terror-stricken. The hours she spent in doctors' offices, the regimen of medication and shots—all this would have been too much for most people to handle. But in serving others she forgot herself, and demonstrated that fear cannot coexist with love.

13

Getting Off the Ground

I could have called this chapter "Discipline Two." Remember that formula?

DELIVERANCE FROM FEAR =
DYNAMISM + DEVOTION + DISCIPLINE.

Discipline has two uses. The first one—the vital need to be disciplined in your spiritual life—I have discussed already. But you also will need to be disciplined in maintaining and executing your overall strategy against fear.

The reason is simple. Think about the individual soldiers in an army. Each is only a man, with a limited amount of strength. Each is probably strangely fearful on the eve of a battle. What gives the army its strength? I submit that the crucial factor is discipline, a dedication to duty that turns a group of individuals into a fighting unit. Did the armies of Rome sweep across the ancient world because they were better equipped or more courageous than their enemies? No. They founded and established the great empire of Rome on the bedrock of an iron discipline. And what about the famous King Harold at the Battle of Hastings—was he defeated by William the Conqueror in 1066 because he lacked swords or armor? No. He lost because his men, in panic, broke their lines at a crucial moment in the conflict. They were undisciplined.

Your discipline can be the deciding factor in the battle against fear. Develop it, and your life will be enhanced. Neglect it, and the fight for a productive and fulfilling life is all but lost.

What I purpose to do in this chapter is suggest a step-by-step program for you to follow.

I emphasize that it isn't a new piece of advice given in addition to the formula. The advice Paul gave to Timothy is wholly adequate to overcome fear; in that sense I have nothing to add to it. But as I said in the last chapter, the three elements of the formula cannot be put into effect one at a time, anymore than you can walk using only one leg. Success in your battle with fear comes by using the three elements in combination. This program is designed to do exactly that, to help you "get off the ground" by applying the Timothy Formula to your own personal situation, and start living that new quality of transformed life that will sound the death knell for your fears.

You are waiting in the departure lounge. You have your boarding card in your hand, waiting for the boarding call. In a few moments you will strap yourself into your airplane seat in anticipation of the takeoff. Before takeoff, I want to ask the question posed at the beginning of this section, a question to which I hope you've already given a firm positive answer: Are you 100 percent committed to making this life-changing journey against fear?

I cannot affirm long or loudly enough that to handle fear you must face reality.

In "Trouble Ahead Needn't Bother you," Jackie Robinson, Brooklyn Dodgers baseball star, recounts an important lesson learned August 19, 1945, the day Branch Rickey, former President of the Brooklyn Dodgers asked him to become the first Negro to play in major league baseball:

> "Mr. Rickey," I said, "it sounds like a dream come true—not only for me but for my race. . . .There will be trouble ahead—for you, for me, for my people, and for baseball."
>
> "Trouble ahead," Rickey rolled the phrase over his lips as though he liked the sound. "You know, Jackie, I was a small boy when I took my first train ride. On the same train was an old couple, also riding for the first time. We were going through the

Rocky Mountains. The old man sitting by the window looked forward and said to his wife, 'Trouble ahead, Ma! We're high up over a precipice and we're gonna run right off.'

"To my boyish ears the noise of wheels repeated 'Trouble-ahead-trouble-ahead. . . .' I never hear train wheels to this day but what I think of this. But our train course bent into a tunnel right after the old man spoke, and we came out on the other side of the mountain. That's the way it is with most trouble ahead in this world, Jackie—if we use the common sense and courage God gave us. But you've got to study the hazards and build wisely. . . .

"God is with us in this, Jackie," Mr. Rickey said quietly. "You know your Bible. It's good, simple Christianity for us to face realities and to recognize what we're up against. . . .We've got to fight out our problems together with tact and common sense."*

I love my brothers and sisters in Christ, and I don't say this as a put-down, but frankly, unreality has paralyzed a large segment of the Christian church in its viselike grip. How often I've heard church members stand up and say, "Jesus saves; He keeps; He satisfies!" while their faces are long enough to suck marbles out of a gopher hole. Others, wearing tense expressions, shout their praises so loudly they remind me of cheerleaders desperately trying to rally supporters whose team is losing the game.

Pretending that everything is okay is not the solution to your fear, even if the pretended behavior is what your friends expect of you. A man who has fallen overboard doesn't think to himself, "I'd better not shout for help; somebody might think I'm in trouble." He yells like crazy until he catches the attention of someone who throws him a life belt. His need

*Norman Vincent Peale, ed., *Faith Made Them Champions* (New York: Prentice-Hall, Inc., 1954), p.238-39.

dictates his actions. And if you have a problem with fear, that's the way it should be for you. Acknowledge it. Bring it out into the open. You don't have to go around your church or office telling your friends about it, but at least don't hide it from yourself.

Step One—Analyze your fear

Once you've got the fear in your sights, take a long hard look at it.

You may find it helpful to set aside an hour or two in quiet solitude, with a notepad, to make sure you have recorded every facet of your fear. Use the categories I suggest in Part 1 of this book. Divide the fear-object(s) from the fear-scenario(s), pinpointing as accurately as you can what persons or events you fear. Decide whether it is a *Wild Wood fear* or a *Big Bad Wolf fear*, or a combination of the two. Become thoroughly acquainted with your fear, just as a skilled hunter becomes thoroughly acquainted with the habits of his prey.

Now turn your attention to the danger on which the fear is based. Is there a difference—a *rationality gap*—between the danger as it really is, and the danger as you perceive it? You may find that a hard question to answer, because levels of danger can be difficult to assess. But try to find out everything you can about the danger. Is that disaster you are so afraid of really likely to occur? How often does it occur to people like you? And what about the results? Is the event you fear going to leave you physically or mentally incapacitated, financially ruined, socially devastated, or just a bit out-of-pocket and a little shamefaced? Believe me, there are many Americans who nourish tremendous fear over trivialities.

It may help to gain a perspective on your own fear by comparing it with the fear of trusted friends. Say you have a teenage daughter about to leave home for the university, and you are terrified something may happen to her. She may get hooked on drugs, compromise her morals, or lose her faith. You will probably know a couple with a daughter in college.

What has been their experience? Is there anything about life at the university that is really dangerous? How do your friends cope with any dangers they imagine their daughter has to face? Are they able to cope with it?

This analysis of your fears and possible dangers may lead you to one of the following conclusions.

First, you may feel your fear reaction is entirely justified. If you are about to undergo major surgery, for instance, you will probably feel fear in anticipation of pain or possible death. You may also fear that you will be unable to provide for your family and loved ones. You have legitimate cause for fear.

Second, you may feel that the danger before you is making you more afraid than it should—in other words, you are suffering from *exaggerated fear*. A lot of women facing major surgery fear rejection through the deterioration of their youthful beauty. It is true that younger women are more likely to attract a certain sort of attention from the opposite sex. But there is vastly more to a person than a shapely figure and a flawless complexion. Fear of aging in that situation is usually *exaggerated fear*.

Third, you may feel incapable of distinguishing the real danger from the perceived danger.

This confusion may arise in two ways. Let's assume that you are about to take a trip to a country in the midst of civil war. Just before you go, you hear there has been a flare-up near the city you plan to visit. How much danger will you encounter? You don't know. You may be in no danger at all. On the other hand, you may be risking your neck! You are frightened because of a lack of information about the danger. And rightly so. As long as you cannot quantify the danger ahead, your God-given faculty of fear will urge you to be cautious.

But imagine now that a reliable authority tells you your destination is completely safe. Fear can no longer be justified from lack of information. Yet you continue to feel scared. You are convinced, in the teeth of evidence to the contrary, that you are going to be blown up or shot down the moment you step off the plane. When someone tries to reassure you by showing you newspaper reports that verify the safety of the area, you refuse to believe the reports. You are incapable of distinguishing the real danger from your perception of supposed danger.

Clearly your problem in the last instance is far more serious. With the best will in the world, you cannot close the *rationality gap* and consequently your view of reality is distorted. You are like a blindfolded man trying to cross a busy highway. If this is your situation, I advise you to enlist the expertise of a good friend, or perhaps a pastor or reliable professional counselor, to provide you with a touchstone—an outside view of your fear that is not blinkered by your faulty perception. If you are crossing that highway, you want to go with someone who can see the traffic!

Step Two—Confront your dangers

The object of the first step is to see your danger as it really is. Until you can do that you will never be able to act effectively against it. Your faulty perception may immobilize you as it immobilized the Israelites when the 12 spies whom Moses had sent to reconnoiter the land of Canaan returned.

> They told him and said, We came unto the land whither thou sentest us, and surely it floweth with milk and honey; and this is the fruit of it. Nevertheless the people be strong that dwell in the land, and the cities are walled, and very great: and moreover we saw the children of Anak there. . . .We be not able to go up against the people; for they are stronger than we (Numbers 13:27,28,31).

You can detect in this passage how faulty perception led these men to overestimate the danger and saddled them with *exaggerated fears*. Only Joshua and Caleb saw the danger in the true context of God's call to them to occupy the Promised Land. But seeing the danger correctly wasn't the same as overcoming it. The danger was still great enough to tempt the Israelites back to the security of bondage and brick making in Egypt. Another move was called for, a move that I am calling the second step of the strategy for winning over fear. Moses wasn't content to see the danger for what it was; when he saw it, he led his people to confront it.

If you haven't already read the biography of Paul J. Meyer, founder of the Success Motivation Institute, I suggest you do it. It's an object lesson in confronting danger.

Paul Meyer started from zero; some people might say he started from below zero. He had no money, no connections, no college degree. Yet by the age of 25 he had built the largest insurance business in history. Two years later he was flat broke, the victim of crooked dealing in the parent company's leadership. At this point his preacher friend and mentor, Dr. William M. (Bill) Hinson, introduced Paul to Jarrell Mc-Cracken, Hinson's old college friend. As a result of that meeting, Paul Meyer joined forces with McCracken, the founder of WORD, then a neophyte and struggling publishing company in Waco, Texas.

When Jarrell McCracken visited Paul Meyer's magnificent Miami home, he chuckled and said, "We can't afford to pay you." Paul offered to come to WORD on a straight commission basis. In no time at all he had put WORD on the map. But his commissions compared favorably with the net profit of the entire company! This was not acceptable to the company, and a parting of the ways resulted. Once again Paul Meyer was left with a family, no position, and no income.

He went to see Bill Hinson, who gave him this advice: "You're at your happiest when you're helping other people move toward their potential. Why don't you start a business designed to help thousands of people in the same way you're already helping a few, face-to-face?"

At first the idea seemed ludicrous. There were any number of ways a project like that could run aground. But Paul Meyer looked coolly at the dangers, and after making meticulous plans, he launched Success Motivation Institute. He now does business in 75 countries of the world, and is the leader of a firmly established, financially sound organization.

Like Moses, Paul Meyer could have let himself be paralyzed by the thought of what might go wrong. After all, things had gone sour for him on previous occasions. He refused to allow previous setbacks to distort his perception with *exaggerated fear*. He confronted danger and planned to knock it out.

Of course, there are as many ways of confronting danger as there are dangers to confront. But these various ways of confronting danger do have a common feature—what we might call "active engagement with the problem." You would be surprised at how often a little effort on the part of the fearing person puts an end to danger. Never let fear fool you into thinking there is nothing to be done. As King Solomon said in Proverbs, "The soul of the sluggard desireth, and hath nothing: but the soul of the diligent shall be made fat" (Proverbs 13:4).

I'll show you how this type of confrontation can work in two areas.

First, with *Wild Wood fear*. You and I both know that life is uncertain, that there are no ultimate guarantees. Almost anything *might* occur in your life. So what does "active engagement" mean in this situation?

The most obvious answer is: precaution. Precaution is the first objection of *rational fear*. It is because you fear your children may catch polio that you take the precaution of having them inoculated. It is the fear of leaving your family destitute that impels you to take out an insurance policy. It is the fear of injury that stops you from driving a car without brakes.

One of the inconveniences of yielding to an *exaggerated fear* is that it drives you to take precautions for which there is no real demand. Fear of injury in an automobile accident is useful if it stops you from driving off in a faulty jalopy, but obstructive if it renders you unable to do any driving at all. That sort of behavior hardly merits the name "precaution." It does not address the danger, only your fear and your distorted perception. You are really running away from the fear-scenario, the experience which, in your heart, you know will stimulate your fear.

Active engagement means taking the bull by the horn, or rather, taking the car by the steering wheel and the controls, and forcing yourself to do what your perception tells you is dangerous but in fact is not. How else will the dynamism that God promises to release in your life strengthen you against fear? Confrontation is vital, just as it was vital for the Israelites to cross the Jordan and enter the Promised Land. Occupation of the land God had promised to them remained only a theory, an idea, until they took positive action to possess it.

But remember, too, that when Joshua led the people over to the Promised Land, he didn't send a telex to all the Canaanite kings inviting them to join in a collaborative effort to fight him! He invaded the land of strong peoples and walled cities one at a time. In the same way, it would be sheer folly for you to attempt the conquest of your fear of road accidents by jumping behind the wheel and heading for the most crowded freeway. The first time it may be enough for you just to get into the driver's seat. The second time you might start the engine. The third time you could put the car in gear and drive a few yards down your driveway. Start with what you can do, and go on to conquer your fear stage by stage.

I strongly recommend that you use this suggested program as a guide in writing out your personal program for winning over your specific fears. Break up your program into a series of small steps that will take you from sitting in the driver's seat to motoring around town.

A program is a form of discipline. It will help you work on your fears consistently. It will give you the means to monitor and measure your success. Stick to it, and it will carry you forward to ultimate victory. It may be awhile before your "Promised Land" is subdued and you can drive happily in the rush hour. That is not important. The point is to progress a little bit every day. That way you build your confidence until you can face what was once an unassailable fear-scenario.

I can think of no finer example of victory over *Wild Wood fear* than the habit pattern of the former treasurer of Haggai

Institute, the late Guy W. Rutland, Jr. I'm sure many businessmen questioned the soundness of his unique generosity. Fear restricted the giving of many of these businessmen who observed Guy with awe. Guy Rutland understood the line attributed to Jim Elliot, the missionary martyred by the Auca Indians in Ecuador: "He is no fool who gives what he cannot keep to gain what he cannot lose." Guy lived as modestly as I do. The difference was he didn't have to. His gift check for Haggai Institute arrived on the first of every month, and even though there were lean times in the trucking business, as in every other business, you could never tell when those times had settled on him by the size or timing of his gifts. He had conquered *Wild Wood fear* in an area of life that terrifies most people.

The second area where "active engagement" can overcome the danger is in *Big Bad Wolf fear*.

What I said about the fear of automobile accidents also applies here. And consider also that the real damage you sustain through rejection (domestic violence and work layoffs excepted) is often limited. "Sticks and stones may break my bones," the old proverb says, "but words will never hurt me." Tackling your fear of rejection by avoidance, therefore, is overkill of an even worse sort than refusing to drive for fear of an auto crash. It stands to reason that the hermit will not be rejected. But who wants to be a hermit?

To illustrate, I am going to take an example from one particular kind of *Big Bad Wolf fear*—the fear of having past misdeeds exposed, a fear that often finds expression in guilt.

I have been involved in literally hundreds of protracted church meetings, but I can only point to two city-shaking revivals. A revival is a movement of God that results in His people getting right with Him, confessing their sins, making restitution, and setting a new course laid down by the Holy Spirit. One such revival was released by the Spirit of God on the little city of Lancaster, South Carolina, in 1949. For the first 12 nights of the meetings, the evangelist did not give an invitation to the audience to make a public decision. Yet people were getting right with God in the quiet of their own homes. It was incredible by normal standards. Some went back to the principal of the high school with their diplomas in their hands and confessed, "We cheated our way through school. We don't deserve this. We want to make arrangements to earn a legitimate diploma."

One man—a deacon, if you please!—phoned the Gulf Oil distributor at two in the morning and said, "Bill, I've owed you $55 since 1929." (That was a princely sum in 1929, believe me.)

Not surprisingly, the distributor barked back to the deacon, "You're drunk. Go back to bed."

"No, I must get this debt settled. I'm coming over to see you."

And he did. Before daybreak the Gulf Oil distributor found the record of the 20-year-old $55 debt owed by this deacon, a debt the distributor had written off as an irretrievable loss years before.

During these same meetings a young woman, later to become my secretary, was working as secretary to Mr. Marshall of the Marshall chain of furniture stores in South Carolina. She said to her boss, "Mr. Marshall, have you heard about the meeting over at Second Baptist?"

"Meeting!" he cried. "H——, that's no meeting—that's a revival! I've had more people come in to pay off bad debts in this last week than I've had come to me in all the years I've been in business. And every time they've said it was because they'd gotten right with God over at Second Baptist."

He wasn't the only one whose attention the revival had arrested. People from out of town would visit and exclaim, "It seems that this whole town is upbeat and smiling." People by the hundreds who had been enslaved by fears of the exposure of past misdeeds were set free. Wherever they could do it without hurting innocent people, they confessed not only to God but to the persons injured. One man was so smitten by grief over a major theft he had committed that he determined to return the money. When he found that the victim of his larceny had long since died, the repentant thief calculated the total amount stolen plus the appropriate interest for the intervening years in addition to a 20 percent add-on, and gave the entire amount to the Lord's work. He couldn't make the full payment all at once, but he added a percentage of the restitution amount to his regular weekly tithe (ten percent of his income) until full restitution had been made.

Of course, you need to bear in mind factors about confession as a form of active engagement against fear. For one thing, your confession must not cause unnecessary suffering to innocent people. You must always avoid this. The principle is, "Confess to whom confession is due." It is neither fair nor honorable to relieve your own fear by loading pain on somebody else. Another factor is this: in neutralizing one danger you may lay yourself open to another. At a highly publicized campus revival in the '60's, a beautiful young coed, convulsed by guilt, confessed to promiscuous relationships with many of the boys. When the revival ended she was hassled by so many of the young men on campus that she left the school with tears and a broken heart to seek peace and anonymity in a distant university.

Step Three—Censor your input

In 1951 a church in Chattanooga, Tennessee, extended a call to me to become pastor. I was 27 and had just finished an extraordinarily happy ministry in Lancaster, South Carolina. One of the few clouds to have crossed my horizon in Lancaster was an incident involving a mean and disturbed man who, for reasons of churlishness and cantankerousness, had been removed by the deacons from a position of church leadership with the unanimous backing of the congregation. I think he would have fought the decision, but since he could not take on the entire congregation, he stopped attending the church and took every opportunity to scandalize its leadership.

I had almost forgotten about the affair until, two days after I had preached my valedictory sermon in Lancaster, the sheriff phoned to tell me he had a warrant out for my arrest. The sheriff was a good friend who was understandably embarrassed. He attended my church regularly on Sunday nights though, regrettably, I never had the joy of seeing him profess faith in Christ. He said, "Preacher, I don't want to come out and serve you this summons, but I'd be grateful if you'd come into my office." This I did as soon as I hung up the phone.

When I arrived at his office he was sitting pensively behind his desk. His crimsoned face and set jaw signaled his embarrassment and his anger at my accuser. The accuser was none other than the disgruntled church member who had taken unbelievable steps to have me arrested and forced out of the ministry. He charged me with defaming his character.

Arrangements, legally circumspect to the last detail, were made for me to enjoy my freedom pending the decision of the grand jury which was to meet several weeks hence. The possible punitive action was not nearly as distressing to me as the thought that this matter inevitably would go before me to Chattanooga, and my new ministry would die aborning. I was certain that no amount of explanation on my part would undo the damage. Worse, I saw the possibility of a termination to my ministry, period.

I had enough other burdens to carry without adding this to my load. And, still worse, Christine, my wife, was on the threshold of exhaustion from the care of our four-month-old, cerebral-palsied son.

I think you'll agree that my situation provided grounds for *rational fear*. At only 27 years of age I was in danger of having my character assassinated and my ministry shot down like a clay pigeon. Yet, my wife can testify, I didn't lose an hour's sleep over it.

How did I handle the situation?

Obviously, I analyzed the danger. And I confronted it head-on with all the means at my disposal. First and foremost, I committed the entire matter to God in prayer. Then I sought the advice of the finest legal minds—churchmen who understood both the law and the Bible. I thus secured my freedom of movement so that the case should not delay my departure to Chattanooga. To ground me, after all, was what my opponent most wanted. As I heard from several people later, he planned "to delay that preacher's move so long he won't have bread on his table."

But I did something else, too. You see, it would have been easy for me to start feeling, thinking, and behaving defensively at best, or guilty at worst. Once a charge has been leveled at you, you can find plenty of people, most of them good and innocent people, who are prepared to entertain the notion that the charge just might be true. It was, therefore, vital for me to protect my mind from negative input. I made a point of not listening to any doubtful criticism. I forced myself to think and act as though the grand jury's throwing out the case as fraudulent was a foregone conclusion.

That's exactly what the grand jury did. In fact, I was advised to sue the man. I didn't. In a short time, I learned he had quit the church altogether and, I'm sorry to say, died prematurely, an embittered and unforgiving old man who seemed to hate the world. But I think I can say honestly that during the whole unpleasant business I never suffered from *exaggerated fear*. And certainly one important influence on that episode was the grip I, by the grace of God, maintained on my own mind—the way I censored input.

What input you need to censor naturally depends on the object of your fear. A nervous investor would be well advised not to dwell on the opinions of the bearish commentators. A woman with breast cancer will more easily win over fear if she refuses to feed her mind on the horror stories that wickedly sensational journalists write about mastectomy. Anyone anywhere will lead a happier life when the environment is surcharged by positive and affirmative feedback from others. The principle is delightfully simple. Every day you are feeding your mind, just as you are feeding your body. If you feed your mind on a junk food diet of depressing, negative, and pessimistic ideas you will end up ravaged by fear.

Perhaps you never thought about that before. Think about it now. A healthy mind is vital for victory over fear. Make it a discipline to put every new idea you receive through the grid of "sound-mindedness." Don't just swallow somebody else's opinion. Exercise a bit of critical judgment. Ask yourself, "What authority does this person have for saying that?" or "Why should all his gloomy predictions apply to me?" You will probably find that most of these unsolicited ideas have very little power over your life. If that's true, why waste time on them? You can't possibly derive any benefit from exposing yourself to them.

So, when you suspect that a book, an article, a film, or a meeting is just going to trouble you with fear, avoid it like you would the plague. Nobody is compelling you. Would you eat a slice of moldy bread? Of course not. Then why should you have to feed your mind on stuff that tastes lousy and makes you ill?

Step Four—Cultivate your love

Your aim in winning over fear is to be able to live as though your fear never existed.

When the ordinary person talks about his "aim" it is understood that he has not yet achieved it. It is hooked up like the last car of a freight train bound for a long period of hard slog through hundreds of miles of mountain terrain before reaching the destination. If he aims to be a millionaire he will expect to spend the first few years in relative poverty. If he aims to conquer Mount Everest he will know there is a price to pay in arduous fund raising, training, and climbing. Looked at in these terms, aiming to win over fear would mean putting off, perhaps for years, the rewards of winning.

Fortunately, for two reasons we are not required to assign this meaning to the word "aim" when we use it to describe our fight against fear.

First, because, as we've already seen, fear is overcome a piece at a time. That is nonsense with regard to wealth or mountain climbing. Either you have become a millionaire, or you have not; either you have reached the summit, or you have not. Of course, I'm not denying there is an element of struggle involved in the fight against fear. But the man who tackles his fear of accidents on the road by driving a little farther each day is *already achieving his aim.* He is conquering fear progressively, as the Israelites did in occupying Canaan.

Second, there is the important matter of attitude. Look at the Israelites. They didn't cross the Jordan merely hoping to find a home on the other side. They didn't say, "Boy, I surely hope those sons of Anak will let us stay here." They crossed over in the assurance that victory was already theirs. Part of the secret of their success was in their assuming the role of victors from the outset. They reinforced the success of the enterprise with a positive mind-set.

You can observe this principle at work in the lives of the New Testament Christians. Read Acts 16 and see what potential fears confronted Paul and Silas on their visit to Philippi. They had hardly begun their work before the rulers of the city had them thrown into prison on trumped-up charges:

> When they had laid many stripes upon them, they cast them into prison, charging the jailor to keep them safely: who having received such a charge, thrust them into the inner prison, and made their feet fast in the stocks (Acts 16:23,24).

What did Paul and Silas do? Did they accept the idea that they were done for? Did they surrender to fear? Just the opposite. "And at midnight Paul and Silas prayed, and sang praises unto God: and the prisoners heard them. And suddenly there was a great earthquake . . . " (Acts 16:25,26). Even in the stocks of a maximum security prison, Paul and Silas knew they were "more than conquerors" through the love of God. Victory was theirs not next month, not even next morning, but right during the very time they were in the stocks.

That means you must stand your aim on its head. Winning over fear isn't something you are going to achieve some day in the far distant future. You already have the victory—if you claim it and act upon it. You already have power over the fear that stops you from driving, socializing, taking responsibility, or whatever. You have it because you are a redeemed child of God*, living by the life-transforming principle of devotion. Why then do you feel as if power over your fear is some dim and distant objective? Well, probably habit! You have thought that way for so long it's hard to break the thought mold. You haven't yet used God's gift of discipline to release devotion and dynamism.

This step—using discipline to cultivate love—is the fourth and final step in your fight against fear.

I've already said that one way of taking this step is to let fear act as a reminder to love. Employ this procedure at every opportunity. But remember, there are other ways of cultivating love, too.

First, consciously push yourself into a new mold. Ask yourself, "How would I think, speak, and act if I had never suffered from this fear?" Write out a few ideas that you can follow up. If you have been afraid of meeting new people, for example, get into the habit of looking at them with smiling eyes while extending a firm handshake. If you so fear financial trouble that your giving has dwindled, resolutely take action to give in the amount and with the regularity God commands.

Second, perseveringly give thanks in faith for your victory over fear. By all means use your quiet time to ask God for strength, but don't fail to thank Him for the extra step you managed yesterday, and for the inevitable victory of your next step today.

Third, see yourself winning over fear. When you think of fear-scenarios, deliberately picture yourself confronting the danger, and in the power of God, subduing the fear and coming through safely. Until now your visualization has all been negative. That's what fear-scenarios are all about! Turn that around, so that fear-scenarios become success-scenarios.

*If you are not a redeemed child of God, turn to Chapter 21 in my book *How to Win Over Worry* to understand what it means to be a redeemed child of God, or write to me at Box 13, Atlanta, Georgia 30370, and I will be happy to tell you how you may be a redeemed child of God and know it.

Fourth, make your self-affirmations work for you in the conquest of fear. Write the affirmations on cards, mount them on frames, attach them to the sun visor of your windshield, place them on the wall, learn them, and repeat them to yourself whenever you have a free moment.

In his book *The Practice of Godliness*, Jerry Bridges of Navigators rephrased the virtues of love in 1 Corinthians 13 in terms of motivational statements:

- I am patient with you because I love you and want to forgive you.
- I am kind to you because I love you and want to help you.
- I do not envy your possessions or your gifts because I love you and want you to have the best.
- I do not boast about my attainments because I love you and want to hear about yours.
- I am not proud because I love you and want to esteem you before myself.
- I am not rude because I love you and care about your feelings.
- I am not self-seeking because I love you and want to meet your needs.
- I am not easily angered by you because I love you and want to overlook your offenses.
- I do not keep a record of your wrongs because I love you, and "love covers a multitude of sins." (Jerry Bridges, *The Practice of Godliness*, NavPress).

If you will make these motivational statements your own affirmations, you will go a long way toward cultivating love and winning over fear.

You repeat self-affirmations every day anyway. Simply change them from fear affirmations to faith affirmations.

Any positive and relevant statement will do—for instance, "Claiming God's power over my thought life, today I shall love and not fear." I recommend that you choose Scripture verses that you can legitimately apply to your special situation. Philippians 4:13 is appropriate: "I can do all things through Christ which strengtheneth me;" or John 14:27: "Peace I leave with you, my peace I give unto you . . . Let not your heart be troubled, neither let it be afraid." To find verses suited to your particular situation, I suggest you dip into the Psalms. Some Psalms, Psalm 91 for example, are a solid source of strength in danger. You will find undergirding help in reading such portions of Scripture out loud when you are tempted to feel afraid. Read them repeatedly until you know them and they have become a part of you.

Finally . . .

Finally, a brief note for you if you suffer a special sort of fear.

I have written this book to help those whose problems arise from a wrong reaction to danger. Obviously, winning over fear will involve the confrontation of danger, but most readers, I think, will discover the danger of which they were so afraid to be much less threatening than they originally perceived it to be.

But what if your danger is acute—acute enough to give you valid reason to believe that while you have been stung badly once, you are almost certain to be stung again?

I think, then, your problem is of a different sort. Of course, you will experience fear—that is only natural. But it is the danger, not the fear, that you need to overcome. Your fear is *rational fear*, fear that's doing its job. And so, hard as it may be for you to believe, it is on your side. Your total experience is not so much one of fear as one of pain. I could here enter some remarks under that heading, but I simply cannot do it justice in the space available in this volume. I have treated the problem fully in the companion volume to this one entitled, *How to Win Over Pain*. If you feel you are suffering this special sort of fear, I urge you to read the companion volume.

Part 4

Flying By Faith

14

Sufficient unto the Day

Have you started to put those four steps into practice? If you have, you are airborne.

Maybe now you would like to take a glance out the window and consider what holds you up. What is the spiritual aerodynamic that supports the structure of dynamism, devotion, and discipline? I haven't majored on it so far; nonetheless it is a principle implicit in practically every chapter of this book. It's called faith.

Faith is the essence of fearing God. Without faith, the Bible says, it is impossible to please Him. God will not accept us on any terms other than those of our total powerlessness and His absolute provision. He has, in Christ, accomplished all that is necessary for our spiritual and material well-being. The most we can contribute to the process is our receptiveness—our "yes"—to the gifts of God, from the day we repent to the hour we are received into glory.

That "yes" must not be spoiled by greed. Greed is the great downfall of the spurious "name it and claim it" theology, and the fund-raising endemic in modern America that treats faith as a form of financial investment. On the other hand, our "yes" must not be delivered so tentatively that it borders on mistrust. We are urged by Jesus to live in straightforward, practical dependence on our heavenly Father:

> Therefore we take no thought, saying, What shall we eat? or, What shall we drink? or, Wherewithal shall we be clothed? (For after all these things do the Gentiles seek:) for your heavenly Father knoweth that ye have need of all these things. But seek ye first the kingdom of God, and his righteousness; and all these things shall be added unto

you. Take therefore no thought for the morrow: for the morrow shall take thought for the things of itself. Sufficient unto the day is the evil thereof (Matthew 6:31-34).

This advice follows the point made by Jesus that a man cannot serve two masters (Matthew 6:24). He must decide whether he is throwing his lot in with God, or with mammon—with the life of faith, or with the covetous pursuit of wealth for wealth's sake.

But as ordinary men and women, this presents us with a problem. We all need at least some material wealth—food, drink, and clothing—and we are not convinced we can rely on God to provide it for us. Reason goads us with the apparently *rational fear* that faith will let us down. At the same time it warmly commends the alternative pioneered by the Gentiles—that if you want a job done you had best do it yourself.

In the end, then, the options open to us in life are two: faith, or fear. We seek first the kingdom, believing that the rest will follow, or we take so much thought for the morrow that today is exhausted in a futile attempt to make the future secure.

I say the attempt is futile because there is no way to predict, let alone counter, the evils that may befall us. The most we can hope for, if we put our trust in material goods, is to accumulate so many of them that our ultimate insecurity is forgotten. But then, isn't faith just as futile? God may be good at reassuring us over ultimate issues—death, salvation, and so on—but when it comes to paying the grocery bill at the end of the week, aren't we better off with mammon?

I answer that with an emphatic "no."

If we don't have everything by faith, we have nothing at all. Faith isn't a means by which we earn extra commissions on our sanctification, nor is it a religious window dressing on prudence. It is the air we breathe. And it is to the shame of Christianity that our churches today are filled with men and women who loftily sing "Holy, holy, holy" on a Sunday morning, but live the rest of the week on the principle of fear. They are too afraid to trust God to guide them with their money, to guide them in their businesses, and to direct them in their relationships, their careers, and their social calendars. They are Christians only in theory. In practice they are atheists.

Jesus challenges us to faith in even the most everyday matters:

> If God so clothe the grass of the field, which today is, and tomorrow is cast into the oven, shall he not much more clothe you, O ye of little faith? (Matthew 6:30).

If I were not convinced that God honored faith for our every need, I would not be writing a book about winning over fear. There is only one principle by which your fear can be eradicated, and that principle is faith. Faith alone is the basis for utilizing the Timothy Formula of dynamism, devotion and discipline. Faith alone opens us to the limitless resources of God's power.

You may be thinking, "If that's true, I wish I had a bit more of it!" Well, it's not a matter of having "more" or "less" faith. You can't measure it in gallons like gasoline. We can only talk metaphorically about "having" it, for faith is essentially something you do, a way of living on the premise that God may be taken at His word. It exists always in the present moment; and as it exists, it overwhelms fear just as a roller covers old paint in a brand new gloss. Faith improves health; it improves relationships; it improves personal productivity; it improves devotional life; it improves self-image and personal influence. It makes all things new.

This book, then, is about learning to live in faith, because faith is the direct opposite of fear.

The now of faith

There is one more point about faith that you should know. I began this book by talking about a fundamental human fear, our fear of the unknown. It is this—our sheer ignorance of what lies in store for us—that makes mammon so appealing. In mammon's ample bosom we find some comfort against the future, not a freedom from fear exactly, but the illusion of being prepared for danger when it comes. We walk into the Wild Wood clutching a pistol.

Outside the realm of faith, that is about as much victory over fear as a person can hope for. There is no way of achieving the ideal, of knowing for certain that the Wild Wood contains only mice and buttercups. Such certainty is withheld even from the Christian. But the Christian has one big advantage over the man without faith: he is required to live only one day at a time. The man carrying his pistol into the Wild Wood is anxious about situations, narrow passes, deep recesses, and dark corners that he has not yet come to. But the Christian is told to "take therefore no thought for the morrow: for the morrow shall take thought for the things of itself. Sufficient unto the day is the evil thereof" (Matthew 6:34).

You might look on that as shortsightedness, "ostrichism." It's not. We are talking about the ancient doctrine of faith in the providence of God.

In the life of faith we live without guarantees, just as the Israelites did in their wilderness journey. We walk in a desert, hardly knowing what lies before us, certain that the environment is incapable of sustaining us. Our insecurity, our fear of the unknown, makes us wish we were traveling not in the wilderness, but across a fertile land where milk and honey were available on demand every day of the year. Yet here we are. We have no food—only a God who leads us on and says, "Trust Me."

What God provides for us in the battle against fear is utterly and completely adequate. But like the manna He gave to the Israelites, it is delivered only in daily rations:

> When the dew that lay was gone up, behold, upon the face of the wilderness there lay a small round thing, as small as the hoar frost on the

ground. And when the children of Israel saw it, they said one to another, It is manna: for they wist not what it was. And Moses said unto them, This is the bread which the Lord hath given you to eat. . . .

And they gathered it every morning, every man according to his eating: and when the sun waxed hot, it melted (Exodus 16:14,15,21).

To win over fear, you must get used to living in the "now" of faith.

God's provision for you in your fight against fear is made today, here, now. The future is in God's hands. He controls it. And He will give you strength for tomorrow when tomorrow comes. Until then you must focus on your present situation. Why do anything else? Precaution is your only way of influencing the future, so when you have taken all sensible precautions, you may as well leave it be. Train your energy on the day, the hour, the moment in which you are living. And as you have need, so God will supply.

By faith, you will win over fear.

15

Lambs to Lions

Reading this book won't deliver you from fear.

Agreeing with this book won't deliver you from fear.

Asking God for deliverance won't deliver you from fear.

You must act. Deliverance starts, proceeds, and finishes with you. Not because God hasn't done everything necessary for your deliverance, but because He will not step in and do what you can do for yourself. He has given you the Timothy Formula—but it's up to you to apply it.

You have read this book through once, enough at least to get the gist of it. Now go back to the beginning and read it through again. But this time do it more slowly, concentrating on those parts which you feel apply especially to you. As you read, jot down on a notepad an analysis of your fear in the terms I have suggested in the opening chapters. In other words, put *Step One* into effect. Then draw up a personalized campaign plan. Make sure that you are attacking your fear on the three fronts indicated in *Step Two*, *Step Three*, and *Step Four*. Find a way of confronting your danger. Adopt a specific policy to guard your input. And organize your lifestyle to cultivate the love of God. State your intentions in the form of a to-do list, and incorporate a comprehensive review of your progress into your daily devotions. If you want to, share your new regimen with someone else who can encourage you and keep you on your toes!

Remember, God has not given you a spirit of fear. He has given you a spirit of power, of love, and of self-control. Organize yourself to receive that gift and your fear will be finished. The perfect love of God flooding into your life casts out fear. It turns you from a lamb into a lion.

Are you ready to begin? If you are—congratulations! Victory is yours!

Other Books by John Haggai

How to Win Over Pain
How to Win Over Worry
New Hope for Planet Earth
The Steward
My Son Johnny
Lead On!

About the Author

His home is Atlanta, Georgia. But his international influence touches millions of people because his field of operation is the world. His journeys have taken him around the world more than 60 times, and he travels over 200,000 miles every year. Dr. John Haggai, truly a world personality, is founder and president of Haggai Institute for Advanced Leadership Training headquartered in Singapore.

John Haggai was born in Louisville, Kentucky, the son of an immigrant to the United States who fled his native Syria during Turkey's harassment of Syria in 1912.

A prolific writer, Dr. Haggai's first book, *How to Win Over Worry*, has been a bestseller since 1959 and is now published in over 15 languages. This was followed by *New Hope for Planet Earth, How to Win Over Loneliness, My Son Johnny*, and *The Steward*. Dr. Haggai credits many of the concepts he has developed in his books to his long-term friendship with Paul Meyer. (Mr. Meyer is a member of the Board of Directors of Haggai Institute.)

Because of his reputation as an informative and captivating speaker, Dr. Haggai has been sought after by a variety of audiences. These include the world's largest Rotary Club; the Kiwanis International Convention; the Institute for Human Development in Seoul, Korea; the Texas Medical Association; international investment bankers on Wall Street; graduate students at Yale University; the Texas Academy of Family Practice; as well as numerous other civic clubs, colleges, and universities on all six continents.

John Haggai's face and his name suggest his East-West ethnic ancestry. To the people of Asia he looks like an Asian, not a Westerner. But it's more than a matter of looks or a name . . . he has an empathy for the people of Asia.

HOW TO WIN OVER WORRY
by *John Haggai*

People need help in overcoming worry and need it desperately. The worry problem is at the root of much domestic strife, business failure, economic crises, incurable sicknesses, and premature deaths—to mention but a few of worry's hazards. Presenting more than a diagnosis, Dr. Haggai shows how God's Word offers the prescription for worry that can rid us of worry's devastating effects forever.

OVERCOMING HURTS AND ANGER
by *Dr. Dwight Carlson*

Dr. Carlson shows us how to confront our feelings and negative emotions in order to experience liberation and fulfillment. He presents seven practical steps to help us identify and cope with our feelings of hurt and anger.

PRIVATE PAIN
Healing for Hidden Hurts
by *Rich Wilkerson*

Rich Wilkerson, author of TEENAGERS: PARENTAL GUIDANCE SUGGESTED, tells us that "Few are exempt from some degree of private pain." Private pain may be emotional isolation, a sense of rejection, guilt, loneliness, depression, or other forms of inner anguish kept hidden from others. A book that offers help and understanding and shows how suffering and pain are the tools in the great Master Sculptor's plan for our lives.

THE PURPOSE OF SUFFERING
Knowing the God Who Comforts
by *Dr. H. Edwin Young*

A recent Gallup poll revealed that the most frequently asked question in America is, "Why do people suffer?" Dr. H. Edwin Young takes the reader through the book of Job for God's answer. He rejects the simplistic doctrines prevalent today that state, "You are suffering because of sin . . . God is punishing you!" and "As a child of God you can have complete health, wealth, and success just for the asking." Instead, he points the way to the sovereign God who alone can comfort us and show us THE PURPOSE OF SUFFERING.